discover
postmodernism

Glenn Ward

D0987572

flash.

Hodder Education

Hodder Education is an Hachette UK company

First published in UK 2011 by Hodder Education.

This edition published 2011.

Copyright © Glenn Ward

British Library Cataloguing in Publication Data: a catalogue record for this title is available from the British Library.

10 9 8 7 6 5 4 3 2 1

The publisher has used its best endeavours to ensure that any website addresses referred to in this book are correct and active at the time of going to press. However, the publisher and the author have no responsibility for the websites and can make no guarantee that a site will remain live or that the content will remain relevant, decent or appropriate.

The publisher has made every effort to mark as such all words which it believes to be trademarks. The publisher should also like to make it clear that the presence of a word in the book, whether marked or unmarked, in no way affects its legal status as a trademark.

Every reasonable effort has been made by the publisher to trace the copyright holders of material in this book. Any errors or omissions should be notified in writing to the publisher, who will endeavour to rectify the situation for any reprints and future editions.

Hachette UK's policy is to use papers that are natural, renewable and recyclable products and made from wood grown in sustainable forests. The logging and manufacturing processes are expected to conform to the environmental regulations of the country of origin.

www.hoddereducation.co.uk

Typeset by MPS Limited, a Macmillan Company.
Printed in Great Britain

Contents

1

postmodernisms

Depending upon how you look at it, postmodernism can be a state of affairs, a set of concepts, and artistic approach or a word to describe aspects of any of these. Though it may be hard to pin down, its broad reach, from arts and culture through to society and politics, makes it a fascinating topic of study.

Postmodernism follows on from modernism, breaking with some aspects but extending others. It sees modernist, Enlightenment values as, at worst, excuses for imperialism, social control and the exercise of power.

Its main themes are:
* an erosion of conventional distinctions between high and low culture
* fascination with how our lives seem increasingly dominated by visual media
* a questioning of ideas about meaning and communication
* a sense that definitions of human identity are changing, or ought to change
* scepticism about the stories we tell to explain 'the human race'.

Introduction

Although postmodernism is often said to have begun in the 1960s, no clear historical line can be drawn. The term gained some currency in the 1950s and 1960s, mainly in relation to the arts, but was much more widespread in the 1970s, when it was first used to describe a new mood of exhaustion in architecture and literature. Continual experimentation and innovation seemed pointless.

Postmodernist style was perhaps most visible in architecture, where some of the failures of the post-war Modern Movement were clearest. In the new, postmodernist sensibility, stylistic pluralism, wit, nostalgia and even fun were the order of the day.

By the 1980s postmodernism was widely accepted as a label for the moment.

Key characteristics of postmodernism

Cultural flattening Modernism is seen as elitist; postmodernism seeks to resist this. Meanings and ideas flow through culture in ways that cannot be accounted for by a high/low model.

Formerly scandalous art works are institutionalized in museums and the academy, or become fodder for popular culture. The Modern Movement's 'shock of the new' is now seen as 'a set of dead classics'.

Knowingness Postmodernism insists on 'self-conscious, self-contradictory, self-undermining statement'. Since few people trust their convictions or believe the world can change for the better, irony is the only option. Some see this as cynicism.

Hybridization Postmodernism swaps purity for new combinations of genres, styles and media.

Intertextuality Postmodernism constantly alludes to, quotes and pays homage to other texts.

Eclecticism Bringing material together from disparate sources overlaps with intertextuality and appropriation (taking materials from one source and reworking them in another context).

All of these practices question modernist ideas of originality. Eclecticism is as much a social as an aesthetic phenomenon: what you listen to, watch, eat, wear and believe may be drawn from the myriad centres of global culture.

Surface effects From the embrace of decorative façades in architecture, to outrageous costume changes in pop performance, the effect of postmodernist images is, according to the American critic Fredric Jameson, 'overwhelmingly vivid' but lacking in depth and 'affect'. Meanwhile, meaning and representation are called into crisis. Language and representation are no longer said to reflect or express reality; there are no truths, only interpretations. 'There is nothing outside the text', and 'it is language which speaks, not the author'. 'Meanings' happen between audiences and freely circulating signs, and are not produced by a reality that exists prior to its representation. 'The dissolution of TV into life, the dissolution of life into TV' (as the French thinker Jean Baudrillard puts it) perhaps remains the clearest example of how our lives are infiltrated by simulacra (copies without originals).

Identity as simulation The fascination with depthless surfaces translates into a view of personal identity as a loose assemblage of cultural bits and pieces. The modernist self becomes an identity constructed in and fragmented by multiple codes and contexts. This 'posthumanist' approach variously presents identity as: hybrid, cyborg-like, fluid, nomadic, in a permanent state of 'becoming', or performative and masquerade-like. Existentialist philosophy saw the self as process more than an essence, but sought authenticity: postmodernist 'subjectivity' is process with authenticity abandoned. Not as bleak as they may sound, postmodernist identities are escape routes from dominant conventions of gender, nationality, ethnicity and sexuality.

Not all of these versions of postmodernism agree with each other. However, all reflect a widespread mood of uncertainty and contradiction. Whether this mood is dissipating or being fended off remains to be seen.

The term 'postmodernism' has been in widespread use for four decades or so, but the story of its spread through culture is fairly complex. Apart from a number of isolated early sightings of the term (some of which we will discuss later in this chapter), postmodernism started life mainly as an academic category concerned with certain developments in the arts, but soon became a descriptive term for all sorts of proposed shifts and changes in contemporary society and culture. To take just one example, it was argued that the world had lost faith in technological progress. Because faith in technological progress was seen as belonging to a specific 'modernist' historical period, the term 'postmodernist' was thought an apt description of our new period of disillusionment. However, by the mid-1980s, postmodernism had blossomed into what can sometimes seem like a catch-all term for just about anything.

By the middle of that decade, postmodernism in many areas (such as architecture, politics or literature) was frequently discussed in late-night television 'culture' slots, radio arts programmes, and middlebrow Sunday newspaper supplements. These discussions often consisted of either agonizing over what sense could possibly be made of a word like postmodernism, or dismissing it outright as a trendy buzzword rapidly reaching its sell-by date.

The deluge of books with 'postmodernism' in their title slowed to a steady drizzle by the 1990s but has not quite dried up today. Heated debate has cooled into sober reassessment, and in some quarters (the art world for instance) the word, if not the issues to which it refers, seems to have been wilfully forgotten. Meanwhile, aspects of postmodern theory have been fully integrated into humanities courses right across the Western world.

So postmodernism persists, to the extent that we might almost say (with a little exaggeration) that it has become part of everyday speech. Certainly the word still appears in the 'culture' sections of newspapers and magazines, and is rife online.

Multiplying meanings

Postmodernism is not, strictly speaking, a school of thought. It is not a unified intellectual movement with a definite goal or perspective, and it does not have a single dominant theoretician or spokesperson.

This is because ideas about postmodernism have been adopted by a great many disciplines, from philosophy to cultural studies, from geography to art history. Each area has produced books and periodicals with their own particular angles on the topic, and each has defined postmodernism in their own terms. In short, postmodernism has proliferated. Taken on board in so many different fields, where it can refer to so many different things, its meanings have multiplied, and the sheer volume of texts it has generated have tended to obscure, rather than clarify, what on earth it is all about. The problem is that what postmodernism might mean in one discipline is not necessarily compatible with what it might mean in another.

Postmodernism has led such a complicated life that it is perhaps more accurate to speak of the existence of several postmodernisms. On the one hand, it continues to circulate in popular culture. On the other hand, it remains a controversial subject. For some, postmodernism is firmly established as a shorthand term for a range of social and cultural transformations. Still others have grown out of it or remain sceptical about its usefulness.

The term 'postmodernism' has long had more than one application.

* an actual **state of affairs** in society
* the **set of ideas** which tries to define or explain this state of affairs
* an **artistic style** or an approach to the making of things
* a **word** used in many different contexts to cover many different aspects of all the above.

These are just four of the ways you can think about what postmodernism is. There are probably others. Of course, it is not so easy to separate these approaches in practice. For instance, if there is such a thing as a postmodern artistic style, a theorist of postmodernism might look at how that style relates to, or arises from, a postmodern condition in society.

Although taking something from all of them, the second approach in the above list is closest to the one adopted by this book. Rather than attempt to offer one all-embracing definition, postmodernism is most fruitfully viewed as a variety of perspectives on our contemporary situation. This means seeing postmodernism not so much as a thing, but more as a set of concepts and debates. We might even go so far as to say that postmodernism can best be defined as that very set of concepts and debates about postmodernism itself.

That said, there are a number of identifiable themes which run consistently through the different versions of postmodernism.

* They propose that society, culture and lifestyle are today significantly different from what they were a century, or even half a century ago.
* They are concerned with concrete subjects such as developments in mass media, the consumer society and information technology.
* They suggest that these kinds of development have an impact on our understanding of more abstract matters, such as meaning, identity and even reality.
* They claim that old styles of analysis are no longer useful, and that new approaches and new vocabularies need to be created in order to understand the present.

Pre-history

Perhaps the biggest problem with postmodernism is the word itself. The prefix *post* means 'after', and *modern* can be taken to mean 'current' or 'up-to-date'. How then is it possible to be 'after the modern'? How can we get a handle on such a paradoxical notion? One thing we can do is look at some of the word's history.

Although postmodernism's boom has been and gone, it has actually been around for a surprisingly long time. The term did have a number of isolated early incarnations, and these make up a kind of 'pre-history' of postmodernism. Before we go on to look at some of them, it is worth remembering that we should not see such 'prehistoric' examples as definitive. To do so can sometimes lead us up blind alleys, because what postmodernism meant *then* does not always sit comfortably with what it means *now*. Having said that, the six examples given below are worth looking at because they do overlap in some interesting ways with today's varieties of postmodernism.

The 1870s An English artist called John Watkins Chapman (1853–1903) used it to describe painting which he saw as more advanced than that of French Impressionist painters like Claude Monet or Auguste Renoir.

1917 The German writer Rudolph Pannwitz (1886–1969) spoke of nihilistic, amoral 'postmodern men' who had broken away from the old established values of modern European civilization.

1947 In his abridgement of the first six volumes of British historian Arnold Toynbee's *A Study of History* (1946), D. C. Somervell suggested that Toynbee's focus on history could be called 'post-Modern'. Toynbee then took it up, and put forward the notion of a 'post-Modern age' following on from the Modern Age (1475–1875). The 'Modern' was regarded by Toynbee as a time of social stability and progress. But since about 1875 Western civilization, with the growth of industrialized cities, has been troubled by social turmoil, anxiety and revolution.

1957 American cultural historian Bernard Rosenberg (1923–96) named as postmodern the new circumstances of life in society at that time. He argued that important social and cultural changes were taking place. These changes included the rise of technological domination and the development of a mass culture of universal 'sameness'.

1964 Literary critic Leslie Fiedler (1917–2003) described a 'post-' culture which rejected the elitist values of high-brow modern art and literature.

1968 American art critic Leo Steinberg (1920–) noticed in contemporary visual art (for example, the early pop art) a change in interest from the representation of nature to the 'flat' representation of man-made images. He called this tendency 'postmodern' because, whereas older kinds of modern art had been concerned with capturing visual or emotional truth, pop art was interested in artificiality.

There are two important areas of overlap between these various 'prehistoric' postmodernisms and the meanings of postmodernism today. The first concerns the notion that we have entered a phase in history with its own unique characteristics. The second concerns an important distinction (but also an equally important mingling) between theories of postmodernism in society and theories of postmodernism in the arts.

Modernity and Enlightenment

Some of our postmodern forerunners spoke about society entering a new phase. They claimed that we were in a historical period with novel features that distinguished it from any other time in history. In particular, it was to be distinguished from the preceding Modern Age, there was a sense of the uniqueness of now. The exact character of this age, as well as the precise dates of its beginning and end, has been described in different ways by historians, but it is often associated with faith in:

* progress
* optimism
* rationality
* the search for *absolute knowledge* in science, technology, society and politics
* the idea that gaining knowledge of the *true self* was the only foundation for all other knowledge.

In debates about postmodernism, these kinds of value are often called 'Enlightenment ideals'. In other words, they are associated with the Age of Reason (or the Enlightenment), which originated in seventeenth- and eighteenth-century Europe, and which quickly influenced all Western thought.

This so-called Enlightenment project or project of modernity is not without its own internal disagreements, of course; it involves as many doubts and disputes as any other historical phase. To this degree it may be something of an overstatement to speak of the Modern Age (in Toynbee's sense of the term) as having, or being, a single project. Nevertheless, the general philosophy of the period is often defined in terms of its belief that progress in society could be brought about through the gradual perfection (through increasing self-knowledge and rigorous intellectual method) of humanity. The upside to it was an investment in universal human rights that ultimately led to the French Revolution and the United States' Declaration of Human Rights. The downside to it is that, in believing that their values should be universally applied, Enlightenment thinkers tended arrogantly to see Europe as the most enlightened and advanced part of the world. Europe was seen as more civilized than the rest of the globe, and this led to the view that other countries and races should be colonized, exploited or 'bettered'. Some early accounts of a postmodernism describe a waning of these values or a radical break from them.

This proposed decline or break also forms an important part of today's debates about postmodernism. It is often argued that today's society has lost sight of these ideals. In direct contrast to the above features of the Modern Age, postmodern society is often negatively associated with:

* exhaustion
* pessimism
* irrationality
* disillusionment with the idea of absolute knowledge.

On the other hand, many postmodern thinkers, rather than regretting the fall of the Enlightenment, have actively sought to challenge its assumptions or have celebrated its supposed decline.

The fragmented world

The social world of postmodernity is often seen as a fragmented, plural one in which no single system of beliefs can or should predominate. In his book *The Postmodern Condition: a Report on Knowledge* (1979), the French philosopher Jean-François Lyotard describes the eclecticism of postmodern life: 'One listens to reggae, watches a western, eats McDonald's food for lunch and local cuisine for dinner, wears Paris perfume in Tokyo and "retro" clothes in Hong Kong: knowledge is a matter of TV games.' Postmodernity thus embodies the current phase of multinational consumer capitalism. Like many other theorists, Lyotard is ambivalent about this 'condition', at one moment calling upon us to 'wage war on totality' in favour of endless cultural differences, and at another bemoaning our 'slackened' culture in which no universal values hold sway.

Lyotard is mainly concerned with the 'legitimation crisis' of postmodernism, which is to say the abandonment of the idea that it might be worth seeking common ground between different bodies of knowledge or belief. We must abandon the search for shared values – knowledge and belief are only 'language games' anyway. Globally applicable standards in matters of taste, ethics or knowledge are Enlightenment fantasies. No 'language game' (e.g. philosophy, science or religious faith) can explain or speak on behalf of other 'language games'. Hence Lyotard defines postmodernism as 'incredulity towards metanarratives' – in other words, scepticism towards theories of everything.

Seeing Enlightenment theories as authoritarian means of producing conformity, Lyotard rejects 'universal' values out of a desire to maximize freedom and creativity: he has expressed concern with the control and ownership of knowledge, and has argued that in order to shift power back from systems to individuals the public should be granted free access to all information. (The age of the internet may perhaps lead to the realization of Lyotard's vision.)

The German philosopher Jurgen Habermas shares this unease about rational systems, and proposes that the products of modernity have so far tended to enslave rather than emancipate people. But unlike the more pessimistic Lyotard he regards modernity as full of promise. According to Habermas, postmodernism is irrational and ethically bankrupt. He argues that a universally agreed-upon framework is possible and necessary for the attainment of universal freedom and justice. He rejects the postmodernist view that human identity is unstable or fragmented and insists on the need to address fundamental, timeless human needs: open and rational conversation between communities can lead to the discovery of commonality beneath superficial differences. Thus the promise of the modern, Enlightenment 'project' needs to be completed, not abandoned.

Modernity and modernization

Another name for the Modern Age is modernity. Modernity is connected to the idea of modernization, or simply the awareness of being – or wanting to be – 'modern' or 'now'. Modernization suggests updating something, or bringing something into line with what are seen as present-day fashions and needs. If we talk, for example, of having our kitchen modernized, we mean that we are having it fitted with the latest equipment and decorated in a more 'now' style (of course, having a 'now' style these days might involve having a very 'tomorrow' (futuristic) or 'yesterday' (retro) style).

Similar processes of modernization can be seen in most walks of life, from medicine to town planning to education to telecommunications. It is, of course, an endless process. No sooner is an innovation put into service than it is modified or replaced by a newer, better model. Hence styles in clothes and kitchens will always be going out of fashion, washing powders will forever be 'new and improved', and employers will always find ever-better ways of 'streamlining' their workforce. Such a dynamic of constant and rapid change has been accelerating, especially since the turns of the nineteenth and twentieth centuries.

In or after modernity?

These and other factors have all been seen as part and parcel of a unique stage in social history – a period featuring many important differences between traditional and contemporary society. To this extent, the society we live in now can be interpreted as the result, or as the intensification, of the key features of modernity outlined above. It seems clear, for instance, that new ways of communicating are still being developed, that cities are continuing to grow upwards and outwards, and that the updating process is at least as rapid as ever.

For these sorts of reason, some versions of postmodernism have seen it not as a break, but as an outcome or extension of modernity. Postmodernism in this case is the latest point in the progress of modernization.

For example, between the 1970s and the 1990s, television was often seen as a kind of symbol for postmodernism itself. With its satellite broadcasts, 24-hour rolling news, channel surfing, live reports from war zones and so on, television can indeed seem like a unique innovation. But it can just as easily be seen as a product of the rise of mass media that began in the final quarter of the nineteenth century. Some of the aspects of television that have recently attracted the attention of postmodern theorists will be dealt with later in this book.

The question of whether postmodernism is a split from an older era, part of an endless cycle of change, or just another aspect of the Modern Age (perhaps with a genuine postmodern period yet to come) has been a focus of considerable debate. Opinions on it depend largely on how the timetables of history are drawn up. They depend on where people draw their lines between and around so-called periods of history. As any theorist of postmodernism would argue, such periods exist more as man-made ways of carving up the past and the present than as real stretches of time with actual, momentous beginnings and endings.

Just as there is no straightforward way of drawing a line between the Middle and the Modern ages, so there can be no clean, objective, distinction between the modern and the postmodern. We can point to no single date and claim that it marks either a chasm or a point of transition between the two periods.

A distinction

If you look back at our six early uses of the word 'postmodernism', you will see that it could be divided into two main categories. On the one hand, there was the concern with postmodernism as a *social* and *economic* event, brought about mainly by the spread of mass industry. On the other hand, there was postmodernism as what we might loosely call a *cultural* matter, a matter of changes in the arts.

In some ways this distinction between the social and the cultural is quite artificial. The two can be said to inform each other to such a degree that, in reality, they cannot be separated. Would you, for example, put television into the cultural or the social category? Again, why should the arts be considered as apart from the social? Despite this, it is a useful distinction to bear in mind when you start looking into postmodernism. For instance, novels that have been called postmodernist (novels by, say, John Fowles, Kurt Vonnegut, Don DeLillo or David Eggars) may be named as such because they reflect or express postmodern social conditions or because they have parallels with some postmodern factor found in other art forms. But they may also be called postmodernist because they can be said to come in an important way after literary modernism. Without having to define literary modernism for now (and this, too, is quite a contentious matter), the point to note is that it is not necessarily the same as modernity in society at large.

Now, as you will have noticed from the above, a distinction can therefore be made between postmodernism and postmodernity.

Technically speaking, the first refers to cultural and artistic developments (i.e. in music, literature, art, film, architecture, and so on), while the second has to do with social conditions and the 'mood' that these conditions give rise to.

Sometimes this distinction has been adhered to in postmodern theory, and sometimes it has not. Nowadays, however, postmodernism tends increasingly to be doing service for both sides.

Postmodernism's elasticity

When people ask what postmodernism is, they often seem to be asking for the word to be used as a name for a single, observable thing. That thing may be an object, a human condition, or whatever. Either way, it is something that is assumed simply to exist. The postmodernism label, it is assumed, can then be unquestionably stuck on to it. The thing can be defined, and we can all go home happy, secure in our knowledge of what postmodernism is.

However, many theorists of postmodernism would argue that things do not really happen that way. They would argue that unquestionably postmodern things are not just going about the world waiting to have their postmodern credentials objectively identified by you or me. To name something (whether a theory, art work or aspect of society) as postmodern is not simply to unearth an objectively existing truth about it. Nothing contains a retrievable 'essence of postmodernism' which you can drag into the light and examine for clues to postmodernism's ultimate nature or genetic code. Rather, if you call something postmodern, you are placing it in a certain category, or framing it in a certain way. You are bringing an idea *to* it, rather than discovering a quality *in* it. In doing so you are ultimately linking it to a set of ideas about the world and our relationship to the world.

So postmodernism is most usefully thought of as an elastic critical category with a range of applications and potential understandings. It is a 'portable' term which enables us to enter a great many ideas about the characteristics of the world today. Some of these ideas have only been hinted at so far, and the rest of this book merely begins the process of unravelling them.

2

issues in 'high' and 'low' culture

Postmodernism challenges traditional distinctions between 'high' and 'low' culture because it often sees these distinctions as matters of taste rooted in social class. It rethinks the relationship between art and popular culture, and between works of art and other consumer goods, suggesting that the 'artness' of objects and images is defined by interpretation and context rather than by any inherent qualities.

Postmodernism has been very influential in many fields, with the initial impact in architecture and literature. It is self-conscious and ironic in its approach to style and representation. Eclectic and pluralist, postmodernists see modernism as just a series of 'past' styles to be plundered.

It really became a force in the art world with the pop art of the 1960s, and has been highly influential in photography, video and installation art. Recent developments have seen a return of interest in questions of 'skill' and 'craft'. The notion of 'meaning', however, remains contentious.

Literature and architecture were particularly important in the early identification of a postmodern 'turn' in the arts. We will find that what modernism has come to mean for architecture is not quite the same as what it has come to mean for literature, and therefore that these two art forms are not always reacting to exactly the same thing. Their individual 'postmodernisms' will inevitably be geared towards their particular requirements. Nevertheless, many postmodern ideas, practices and debates are shared across the arts, and this allows us to make some generalizations. Pastiche and eclecticism, for example, have been seen as common artistic strategies within postmodern culture at large. Such practices participate in a blurring of the high/low culture divide that is often taken as a key feature of life in the postmodern age.

The critic Andreas Huyssen has suggested that modernism in the arts defines itself as necessarily outside of, and superior to, the rest of culture and society. Postmodernism, on the other hand, crosses the great divide that modernist art and criticism once tried to place between themselves and mass culture. For various reasons, that supposed split between high and low has become less and less relevant to many artists and critics since at least the 1960s. For Huyssen, postmodernism represents a rejection of modernism's 'relentless hostility to mass culture', and moves towards a new situation in which 'the pedestal of high art and high culture no longer occupies the privileged space it used to'. This means that while the role of the arts is, for Huyssen, to maintain a critical stance towards contemporary society, they no longer do so from an imagined position of superiority.

Postmodernist arts have their feet more firmly on the ground and recognize that they share the same world with all other aspects of cultural life.

The demolition of modernist architecture

If you have visited a shopping centre built at some point in the last quarter of a century, there is a good chance that it had at least some of the following characteristics:

* a mixture of architectural styles from past times
* a mixture of styles from different places
* numerous ornamental, decorative or pictorial features
* lots of play between different surfaces, materials and colours
* a high degree of 'fakeness'
* a high degree of 'referencing' (as well as referring to the styles of different times and places, the exterior of the building might echo the shapes and materials of the surrounding area).

All of these features can be described as aspects of 'classic' or 'early' postmodernism. They represent a departure from the rules and conventions of modernist architecture, but appeared to have become new architectural conventions by the early 1990s.

Modernist buildings, generally speaking, are equally easy to identify. Think of any large grey office block, factory, or housing development constructed between the 1950s and the mid-1970s, and you will probably have in mind an example of high modernism. It is likely to feature the following:

* repetition of a simple shape
* uniformity of design
* complete lack of frills
* harsh, industrial-looking materials
* a flat roof
* dominance over the surrounding environment.

The contrast between this and your nearby out-of-town leisure complex is probably quite stark.

Some modernist edifices have become part of our cultural heritage. In Great Britain, for example, the Twentieth Century

Society campaigns to preserve significant examples of architecture from the period since 1914. The Tate Modern, on London's Thames Bankside, reimagines a modernist power station (designed by Gilbert Scott) as a museum of modern art. Yet many other examples are now being pulled down, associated as they often are with vandalism, 'concrete cancer', and the misery of living in an anonymous box in the sky. One of the first major demolitions of a modernist development took place in 1972, when the Pruitt-Igoe housing project (completed in 1955), was declared uninhabitable and was subsequently dynamited by the city of St Louis, Missouri.

It can be hard to believe that the modernist style was once considered the future of urban planning. Yet the originators of this style saw themselves as part of a genuinely utopian impulse. They really believed that they could make the world a better place, that modernism could play a major part in the improvement of human life.

The Modern Movement

The Modern Movement in architecture is generally identified with a small number of European and American architects working early in the twentieth century: Ludwig Mies van der Rohe, Walter Gropius, Le Corbusier and Frank Lloyd Wright. Their ideas rapidly spread on a global scale. Many of the techniques, as well as the appearance, of their buildings were adopted by architects all over the world, becoming the familiar International Style which we caricatured above. Although there are differences between their ideas, the main thrust was a belief in:

* *Novelty*. It is necessary to be 'up to date'. Architects should express the spirit of the modern, industrial age, and not be tied to the past. It should make maximum use of new building materials and methods. Buildings should be streamlined, *rational* machines. Housing should be based on the same design principles as factories and automobiles. Modern cities should be designed to accommodate speed.
* *Progress*. Humankind can escape from misery only by shedding the past and embracing the age of the machine

and mass production. Modernity is technological progress; industrial manufacturers and machine designers are engaged in a search for universal harmony and perfection. Architecture should participate in this evolution towards a bright, hygienic, efficient society.

* *Heroism*. Modernist architects see themselves as the godlike creators of a brave new world. They have privileged access to the keys to the advancement of civilization, and so they draw the blueprints of the future.

* *Purity*. This utopian vision is to be achieved through the strictest of means. Buildings are to be reduced to their purest forms. Their beauty lies in their function, simplicity, rationality, newness and unity.

In 1908 the influential Austrian architect Adolf Loos (1870–1933) declared that 'ornament is crime' and reasoned that 'the evolution of culture marches with the elimination of ornament from useful objects'. Written in part as an attack on the then-popular Art Nouveau, some of Loos' claims appear elitist and excessive today, especially in light of his assertion that ornament is the 'degenerate' and immoral province of the criminal mind. Yet Loos' view that unnecessary decoration merely serves fashion (and therefore near-instant obsolescence) may echo contemporary criticisms of design 'styling' as a handmaiden of environmentally unsustainable over-consumption.

So what went wrong?

Modernist architects arguably tended to be uncompromising in their attempts to break with the past and forge a brave new world of clean, disciplined order. They had principles. They were committed to producing a democratic architecture for all. The problem was that they became authoritarian and dogmatic, presuming to tell the 'masses' what was good for them, and attempting to fit them into abstract, rational systems. Le Corbusier wanted homes to be 'machines for living', but most people don't want to live in machines. Nor do most people live by Mies van der Rohe's dictum that 'less is more'. While modernists loathe 'unnecessary' decoration, many people find decoration entirely necessary. One defence of postmodernism is that it simply tries to accept this. It replaces modernism's functionality, rationality and purity with more democratic, less elitist playfulness.

Plural coding

In the 1980s the architect and theorist Charles Jencks (1939–) praised postmodernist architecture for its ability to go beyond modernist elitism. Modernist ideas aimed to strip architecture of ambiguity and connotation. They stated that a building should carry no associations outside of its own magnificent declaration of modernity. Jencks calls this aspect of the modernist ideal univalence. What he means by this is that buildings were supposed to have a single meaning. For example, the International Style preferred buildings to be structured around the repetition of a simple geometrical formula.

One problem with this was that modernist buildings often failed to give pleasure to their users. Against this, Jencks proposes that postmodernism is multivalent (has many different meanings) or plural coded. That is, it is deliberately open to many different interpretations. Instead of imposing a single meaning, formula or presence on anyone, postmodernist buildings are more freestyle and allow for the pleasures of finding associations and making connections.

The function of postmodern architecture

So postmodern buildings are collages of different visual styles, languages or codes. They allude at once to local traditions, popular culture, international modernism and high technology, yet refuse to let any one of these elements become dominant. Jencks argues that by mixing and mismatching in this way, plurally coded architecture opens itself up to a wider audience. It is a form of 'dissonant beauty' which, full of vitality, ambiguity and irony, defines different functions according to the needs, tastes and moods of different social groups. It speaks in many accents in order to engage as many 'readers' as possible, all of whom will be able to read the language of the building in their own terms, relating it to their own knowledge and experience.

In this way postmodern architecture is a democratic 'juxtaposition of tastes and world-views' which responds to the fact that we live in what Jencks sees as a pluralistic, cosmopolitan 'culture of choice' rather than one of enforced sameness. This theme of cultural diversity occurs frequently within postmodern theory and practice.

Some criticisms of postmodern architecture

Some critics have seen postmodernism as a failure of nerve on the part of architects. They have regarded it as a decline in standards, a collapse of the artistic imagination, a conservative appeal to the lowest common denominator. Although postmodernist buildings do embrace the latest construction techniques and materials, their designers have lost their bottle and run out of revolutionary spirit. Swapping their moral and aesthetic responsibilities for easy populism, they no longer see their activity as vital to the creation of a better tomorrow.

One reason for this is that architects are married to commerce. Another criticism is that the more progressive postmodernist principles are mostly applied only to places of business, leisure and/or shopping. Housing design remains as unimaginative as ever. Postmodernism is therefore just a way of trying to get people to spend longer at the shops. It is therefore regressive rather than progressive, reactionary rather than radical. Jencks distinguished between:

* *Straight revivalism*. Buildings in this category are seen by Jencks as reactionary or conservative. Any building that is new but looks old fits this description.
* *Radical eclecticism*. The kind of architecture which Jencks puts into this category mixes up styles and references in an ironic way. By placing different styles together it effectively puts buildings in quotation marks, expressing a more critical attitude both to tradition and to architecture itself.
* *Deconstructivism*. More recent deconstructivist architecture has taken the critical spirit of Jencks' 'radical eclecticism'

into even more adventurous – some might say frivolous – territory. Influenced by the ideas of the philosopher Jacques Derrida, and replacing 'form follows function' with stylistic excess, it combines hi-tech materials and methods with postmodernist pluralism and a collage-like sense of design.

* *Complexity and chaos*. In the 1990s Charles Jencks found new inspiration – and confirmation of his ideas – in chaos theory and fractal geometry at the outer shores of physics and mathematics.

Another critic, Fredric Jameson (1934–), has found a similar two-part categorization within the entire field of postmodern culture. He distinguishes between:

* *Pastiche*. Echoing Jencks' view of 'straight revivalism', Jameson sees postmodernism as an art of pastiche that merely mixes references in a hollow, empty spectacle. Pastiche, for Jameson, revels nostalgically in past styles, but shows no understanding of history and no desire to look forward.

* *Parody*. Seen by Jameson as more common to modernism, this is mimicry of old styles again, but unlike mere pastiche it mocks rather than merely plunders from tradition. Like Jencks' 'radical eclecticism', it has a critical edge.

Literature: mind the gap

Modernism within the institutions of the arts often rests on ideas about its relationship with low, mass or popular culture (for the sake of convenience, I will use these three terms interchangeably). Many versions of modernism present high and low culture as two very distinct spheres: there might be degrees of influence from one to the other, but they are essentially worlds apart.

In books like *For Continuity* (1933), F. R. Leavis sketches a view of a discriminating, minority culture which is the standard-bearer of all that is artistically and morally proper. Leavis proposes that a small handful of English, American and European writers – including

Shakespeare, Dante, Ezra Pound, T. S. Eliot, Virginia Woolf and James Joyce – represent the 'finest consciousness of the age' and he sees it as the job of critics like himself to promote their superior works. The parallel here with the arrogant self-perception of the modernist architects is quite clear: both see themselves as having superior insight into what is best for people; both think that they know what kinds of art people ought to have.

Although the writers championed by Leavis are quite diverse, he argues that what they all have in common is a rejection of over-sentimental subject-matter and over-pretty writing styles. Again there are parallels here with modernist architecture's hatred of the frivolously decorative. Leavis sees his literary hall of fame as characterized by intellectual rigour, subtlety and wit. When he discusses writers of the modern period, Leavis makes much of the fact that they are in touch with the language of the contemporary world. However, the point of this concern with everyday life is not to celebrate or participate in it but to subject it to criticism. In Leavis' view the role of modern literature is to oppose modern society and the cliché-ridden (and often 'Americanized') products of its mass media. Elite, minority culture must constantly be on its guard against the spread of Hollywood, advertising, 'potboilers' and other manifestations of facile popular culture. Film is a particularly disturbing influence because it mesmerizes its audience with cheap and easy pleasures.

On this view, the mass art of the industrial age is characterized by commercialism and standardization, and these pose a serious threat to art's single-minded pursuit of timeless values. The modern world distracts people with so many forms of mindless entertainment that they are tempted away from art's traditional, more authentic standards.

By contrast, it is often argued that postmodernism tests the boundaries between what gets called high and what gets called low culture. It asks us whether such distinctions are still valid today (if they ever were), and it asks us to question the grounds on which such distinctions are made. It recognizes that contemporary society offers a vast range of different forms of entertainment, but it is less concerned with defending the 'ivory tower' against them.

The postmodern mood

Around the late 1960s there was much talk of 'the death of the novel' or, as the American author John Barth described it, a 'literature of exhaustion'. At this point the traditional techniques of fiction suddenly seemed obsolete or irrelevant. The complexities of the modern age were impossible to capture in a conventionally 'realist' style, while more 'experimental' or avant-garde ways of writing seemed either elitist, burned out or pointless. Writers of this period therefore faced a dilemma: on the one hand, to find a new 'voice' appropriate to the era of mass communications; on the other hand, to appeal to a popular audience, without at the same time resorting to narrative clichés (e.g. neat endings, logical sequencing of events, cause-and-effect explanations). This was difficult enough in itself, but there was also a feeling that all the good ideas had been used up. The 'great' modernists like Proust or Kafka seemed age-old, worthy but dusty exhibits in a museum.

Though she uses the word 'camp' rather than 'postmodernism', Susan Sontag's *Against Interpretation and Other Essays* (1967) represents an early attempt to define this new sensibility. Sontag notes that not only has the high/low distinction become 'less and less meaningful', but 'the new sensibility is defiantly pluralistic; it is dedicated both to an excruciating seriousness and to fun and wit and nostalgia. It is also extremely history-conscious; and the voracity of its enthusiasm (and of the supercession of these enthusiasms) is very high speed and hectic.' In this context wit, pluralism and nostalgia became the order of the day.

This mood of exhaustion was a common feature of postmodernism as it was formulated in the 1970s and 1980s. Fredric Jameson summed it up well in 1983: 'the writers and artists of the present day will no longer be able to invent new styles and worlds ... only a limited number of combinations are possible; the most unique ones have been thought of already.'

As in the case of architecture, pastiche was one of the tactics for dealing with these problems. It may not be possible to make brand-new, heroic statements, it was argued, but you can at least take existing forms apart and recombine the pieces in enterprising ways. The postmodern text is openly assembled from different genres and styles. A review in the music magazine *Wire* puts it well: 'genius lies in the poise and skill of the blend rather than in the breathtaking innovation of the ingredients'.

A related practice is eclecticism. As we saw with architecture, this involves openness to a wide range of forms and devices. Postmodern artists can switch between genres at will, without appearing to privilege any. While it is impossible simply to invent a new style out of the blue, it is equally impossible to avoid having a style. Regardless of how resourceful they may be, artists are always working within pre-existing cultural languages and conventions. Eclecticism means throwing these together, reshuffling the cards. For artists in this vein all of culture is there to be plundered, irrespective of high/low distinctions.

Metafiction

A novel can be described as 'metafictional' when it wears its artificiality on its sleeve. As defined by Patricia Waugh in *Metafiction: The theory and practice of self-conscious fiction* (1984), a work of this kind knowingly lays bare the conventions of fiction, and draws attention to the language(s) and literary style(s) it uses. In short, it is fiction about fiction. As Waugh puts it, such works aim 'simultaneously to create a fiction and to make a statement about the creation of that fiction'.

As an example, Waugh quotes Italo Calvino's *If on a Winter's Night a Traveller* (1981): 'The novel begins in a railway station ... a cloud of smoke hides the first part of the paragraph.' In this sentence we are reminded of the novel as a novel (as a culturally specific type of writing, and as a physical object). The 'paragraph' it refers to is both in our 'real' world (is part of the actual text we are reading) and is part of the fiction. Several levels or versions of 'reality' tumble over each other, all of which end up seeming fictional.

In these ways postmodernist metafiction questions realism from within: it does not pretend to offer transparent windows on the world, 'slices of life', or illusions of 'authenticity'. By drawing attention to its own status as an artefact, it instead admits that it can offer no objective, complete or universally valid representations.

Self-consciousness

A central feature of postmodernist art forms is the interrogation of their own conditions of existence. This produces ironic effects. As well as using language, postmodern fiction discusses the processes of language. As well as being part of a genre, it talks about genre. As well as presenting us with stories, it asks us to consider what stories are made of.

So things like irony, pastiche, plural coding and eclecticism can seem like ways of having your cake and eating it. And postmodernism can seem to mean not really meaning anything. But if postmodernism puts messages in quotation marks (the poststructuralist thinker Jacques Derrida would say it puts them 'under erasure'), that's because it is by definition self-conscious and self-critical. And that can be a serious business. For the postmodern text constantly asks: How do I produce meanings? How can I offer a 'true' representation of reality? For whom, and from what position, do I speak?

The cultural mix

Consider:
* Advertising has become a new art form. Many television, cinema, internet and 'mobile device' forms of advertising are now more imaginative, vibrant and exciting than much high art.
* Many commercials also make reference to the world of art, but a lot of art equally makes reference to the world of advertising. What's the difference between them?
* What is popular culture anyway? How many people a year need to visit your national museum of modern art, and buy postcards of the art from the museum shop, before it can be called popular?

Many commercials use classical music. Many film soundtracks (particularly horror films) are indistinguishable from experimental modernist music. Many of us are comfortable in several different musical worlds. We are not usually restricted to just one taste. We often organize our own MP3 playlists which happily mix any number of 'levels' or genres of music, or identify our own idiosyncratic musical genres. Modernist critics might once have tried to tell us what we ought and ought not watch, read and listen to, but most of us are much more eclectic (and much less puritanical) than that; we consume a very diverse range of goods offering many different experiences.

On our home entertainment systems and computers the whole of world culture seems to be at our fingertips. The media can appear as placeless imaginary spaces which refuse to make clear distinctions between things. Adverts for ice cream and sun block interrupt art history programmes. Moving into different realities can be done at the push of a button or click of a mouse. Everywhere you look, different, perhaps contradictory, messages, images and ideas jostle for attention.

In this new media domain, anything can go with anything, like a game without rules. Or, at least, you can make up your own rules. Culture can no longer be administered; there is no legislation about what can and cannot be consumed. Modernists would bemoan this as a slackening of aesthetic criteria. Postmodernists would agree, but would say 'good thing too'. They would ask, exactly whose criteria were they in the first place? And why should anybody have taken notice of them?

A more critical eye would say that, actually, censorship and surveillance are stronger than ever, so that cultural access is nowhere near as free as postmodernism likes to claim. Hierarchies of taste and genre exist throughout the cultural industries, despite postmodernism's wishful thinking.

Flattening the hierarchy

Some recent writing on postmodernism has argued that the high/low model is no longer an appropriate way of looking at things. The map of cultural life has been redrawn. In fact, postmodern culture is this new map. There is, for example, no self-evident reason why Bach should be seen as better than Bacharach. This is not to say that they are the same, just that they are equal. Everything swims in the same social sea of signs, images and meanings.

This might imply that supposedly objective statements about quality (e.g. 'That's rubbish') are really subjective statements about personal preference (e.g. 'I don't like it'). However, postmodernism also insists on blurring any distinctions between the cultural and the individual; 'personal' taste is always therefore culturally determined. The classic, hugely influential work on the sociology of taste is Pierre Bourdieu's *Distinction: A Social Critique of the Judgement of Taste* (1984). Bourdieu argues that taste is an expression of social class difference: 'taste classifies and it classifies the classifier. Social subjects, classified by their classifications, distinguish themselves by the distinctions they make.'

A central aspect of the supposed collapse of the 'high/low culture' distinction is the institutionalization and popularization of avant-garde objects and practices. Examples include the phenomenon of the modern art museum as tourist attraction (such as the Pompidou Centre in Paris, the Tate Modern in London, the Guggenheim museum in Bilbao), and the broadcast in 2004 of John Cage's *4'33* (four and a half minutes of performed 'silence' conceived in 1952) on BBC Radio 3.

While such examples suggest a levelling of the cultural playing field, they can also be said to typify mass culture's recuperation or co-optation of material originally resistant to commodification and market forces.

Visual art

Any attempt to define postmodernism as simply a style or period is unlikely to work. There is no single point at which postmodernism springs into being, and it is hard to find a contemporary approach to art that does not share ideas with much earlier twentieth-century work. Another difficulty is that modernism itself tends to resist simple summary. In the first place, it was manifested differently in different countries and movements. Add to that the fact that modernism is still in the process of being redefined in retrospect by postmodernism, and it is clear that the proposed differences between the two are far from cut and dried. The important thing to remember is that being 'post' doesn't have to mean being 'anti-': postmodernism is usually a critical dialogue with modernism, not a rejection of it.

Make it new!

Most descriptions of modernism in art tend to date it from the mid to late nineteenth century, with the development of Impressionist and Post-Impressionist painting in France (Manet, Monet, Degas, Gauguin). This is often described as the beginning of a great experimental period in art, a period in which art pursued new goals and eventually broke free from all traditions of representation. In this simplified view of events, the Impressionists triggered a break from the past in which art learned to turn away from realistic styles of representation and move towards more abstract forms of expression.

In this revolution, art progressed by means of 'heroic' experimentation – the shock tactics of the 'tradition of the new' – towards a position of highly self-conscious art for art's sake. The idea behind this was that art should become valid on its own terms, without having to have any obvious relation to the visual world. Via the innovations of Cubism (starting with the work of Pablo Picasso and Georges Braque, around 1907) and Abstract Expressionism (most often associated with American painting of the 1940s and 1950s by Jackson Pollock, Mark Rothko and others), along with many other movements, modernism is sometimes said to culminate in certain highly reductive (minimalist) art forms of the 1960s and early 1970s.

A brief history of postmodernism in the art world

The term 'postmodernism' first gained widespread use in the art world around the beginning of the 1980s. Although its accuracy as a description of the art receiving attention at that time was sometimes fiercely debated, it was generally agreed the term did at least signal that important changes were taking place in art.

Up until that point international art journals and large collections of contemporary art had been full of rather austere stuff. Although there had always been maverick presences around, the art that tended to be taken seriously by the 'official' (mainly New York–centred) art establishment was generally quite cerebral and dry. Various forms of minimalism in the 1960s and 1970s, for example, reduced sculpture and painting to the simplest forms and processes (bricks, cubes, slabs, grids, squares, flat fields of colour). Much conceptual art of the same period began to appear similarly unseductive: monochrome photographs juxtaposed with deadpan text, holes made in gallery walls and artists performing endlessly repetitive 'actions' were the order of the day. This was all taken as a negation of the progress of art, with minimalist and conceptual art seen as a dead end; there was nothing new left to do. Art was left in an endgame situation; artists could choose only to retread art's earlier steps or to play with its left-overs.

Hence at the beginning of the 1980s it became newly fashionable to do huge, splashy paintings of *things*. Starting in Germany and Italy, representations of the human figure made a return, and in the context of an economic boom for the art world, a number of prominent young, usually male, North American artists (such as Eric Fischl and Julian Schnabel) made fortunes painting them. This early version of postmodernism was associated with a pluralist, 'anything goes' attitude and an obsession with the past. Old styles and techniques were reworked and artists quoted from the work of other artists. Abstract art was still pursued – in a movement known briefly as 'neo-geo' – but this had a more ironic, tongue-in-cheek edge than was usually expected of abstraction. As in the case of postmodernist architecture, art became more playful and even, on occasion, entertaining. Although the new interest in representation was welcomed by some critics, others (such as Robert Hughes and Donald Kuspit) complained about the lack of skill or feeling in the new figurative painting.

Others suggested that the return to painting revealed a sell-out to commerce and a betrayal of the avant-garde, modernist imperative to be culturally progressive, challenging and experimental.

More cautious assessments suggested that ideas about progress, radicality and originality had been myths in the first place and were no longer valid in a complex, media-saturated society. Postmodernist painting could be seen as simply making the most out of the collapse of these myths, or as negotiating with the history and meanings of easel painting in intelligent, ironic ways. The new painting could be seen not as a betrayal but as a lively engagement with modernist ideas. It tested the assumptions of once-dominant critics and beliefs; it raised important questions about what it was that art was now supposed to do, and about how it was meant to do it.

More complex ideas about postmodernism quickly infiltrated the art world. Next to painting, photography and media-based work regained the limelight in the mid-1980s by seeming to provide a more clearly political postmodernism. A number of artists working in this field were hailed for making a specifically feminist intervention in postmodernism, Barbara Kruger, Sherrie Levine and Cindy Sherman chief among them. Others gained notoriety for producing three-dimensional pieces based largely on arranging shop-bought goods, notably Jeff Koons and Haim Steinbach: these were sometimes known as 'simulation' artists. A related approach was appropriation or image scavenging; well-known examples include Sherrie Levine's photographs of photographs by famous modernist photographers, and Richard Prince's 'rephotography' of cigarette advertisements.

The question for postmodernism now was not, as it had been at the beginning of the decade, whether the progress of art had withered away, but how artists should respond to the expansion of consumer culture. From some perspectives, mass media and commodities were seen as the instruments of a corrupt capitalist system. If art was to have any purpose in the contemporary world, it had to set itself up in opposition to this system. How could art subvert (or even compete with) the power of the media?

How could artists oppose the world of commodities without producing luxury goods themselves?

In order to answer these questions, it became necessary to reforge the links between contemporary art, the conceptual art of the 1970s, the pop art of the 1960s and beyond. It also seemed necessary to examine the work of a number of predominantly European postmodern theorists. The work of the French thinker Jean Baudrillard (1929–2007), for example, was often used in the service of the more media-conscious brands of postmodern art, and became something of a cult among artists and art students in the 1980s. Indeed, Baudrillard was for a while nominally on the editorial board of the influential American periodical *Artforum*. Baudrillard briefly became the unofficial, and unwilling, spokesman for what became known as appropriation and simulation art.

Postmodernist approaches to art-making include:

* *Conceptual art*. Conceptual art comes in many forms, but usually involves work in which, to quote the critic Lucy Lippard, 'the idea is paramount and the material is secondary, lightweight, ephemeral, cheap, unpretentious, and/or dematerialized'.
* *Neo-geo*. Combining a minimalist abstract aesthetic with references to popular culture and commodities.
* *Appropriation and simulation*. Informed by the theories of Baudrillard and others, this involved reproducing or copying works by other artists.
* *Trans-avant-garde*. An Italian movement that ironically embraced traditional materials, fanciful subject matter and decorative elements.
* *Neo Expressionism*. Crude, seemingly quickly executed figurative paintings from Germany. Full of references to German history and culture.
* *Eclecticism*. Many artists worked with images appropriated from 'high' and 'low' culture and combined (or juxtaposed) them in a range of styles.
* *The return of craft and skill*. In postmodernism, no one believes in art any more, so craft skills have filled the vacuum.

* *Relational art.* An outpost of conceptual art, relational art was originally identified by the French critic Nicolas Bourriaud in 1998. Bourriaud defined *relational aesthetics* as 'a set of artistic practices which take as their theoretical and practical point of departure the whole of human relations and their social context, rather than an independent and private space'.

Modernism and the autonomy of art

There are a number of widespread beliefs about art. One is that artists dedicate their lives to their art without any ulterior – especially commercial – motive. Another is that artists have unique insight into things. Finally, we often assume that art is somehow timeless. All of these beliefs suggest that art exists in a realm outside of ordinary life. Modernism similarly believes that art is essentially independent and self-governing.

Although this idea of the autonomy of art has been expressed in many different ways, one of the most common is to propose that works of art are intrinsically different from all other sorts of objects. They are governed (if they are governed at all) by rules and interests not found elsewhere, and they provoke special kinds of responses in their audience. Art does not have to justify itself economically, politically, morally, or in terms of its use. It is free from social convention.

One of the most influential statements of this attitude – and the one against which postmodern art and theory most often pits itself – is the work of the American art critic Clement Greenberg (1909–94). Greenberg is known for a number of essays and reviews published in art journals between the late 1930s and the mid-1960s. Two of his best-known pieces, published in the left-wing arts journal *The Partisan Review* are 'Towards a Newer Laocoon' (1940) and 'Avant-garde and Kitsch' (1939).

'Towards a Newer Laocoon'

According to Greenberg, every historical age has a 'dominant art form', and between the seventeenth and mid-nineteenth centuries the dominant art form was literature. This means that literature became the prototype which all other art forms tried to imitate. For example, nineteenth-century salon paintings tried to tell sentimental, melodramatic tales and, in doing so, they were aspiring to the condition of literature.

In Greenberg's view this is an artistic crime. The aspiration towards literary effects in painting and other art forms is a lamentable 'confusion of the arts'. In this confusion, there ceases to be any reliable standard by which artists and critics can make judgements about quality. The aesthetic worth of a painting is a question that can be framed only in relation to the specific properties, conventions and history of painting itself. To look at a painting's ability to tell a story or to imitate a three-dimensional object is to fail to look at it on its own terms. A painting is a painting; it is not a book or a sculpture.

This argument rests on the belief that the various art forms possess – or else should achieve – characteristics of their own which separate them from all other art forms. Greenberg insists that modern art progresses through the struggle of artists to boil their art down to its barest essentials and thus to achieve genuine quality. He calls this progressive refinement a process of rigorous self-criticism.

In these ways, paintings stopped trying to fool people. Instead of pretending to be stories or windows on to another world, they called attention to the fact that they were just flat surfaces made of paint on canvas.

Thanks to this new emphasis on materials – the integrity of the support, the resistance of the medium – painting triumphed over all the other arts. It most successfully defined its own unique essence, and, in doing so, it no longer had to justify itself. Like objects of nature, paintings were now their own justification and reward.

'Avant-garde and Kitsch'

Greenberg implied that in order to enter the space of art you must unburden yourself of social, political, practical and moral baggage. All of these things only hinder the perception of art as art. He notes that art is always surrounded by money, and that modernism was related to the expansion (in the middle of the nineteenth century) of an affluent middle-class market for art. But for Greenberg economic and social factors such as the existence of a system of patrons, galleries and collectors within a privileged class do not detract from the purity of the modernist enterprise – in fact, they simply create favourable conditions in which an autonomous art can flourish.

'True' culture is under constant threat from kitsch. There are two meanings of kitsch in Greenberg's essay. On the one hand, it is a sentimental sort of pseudo-art which rips off the products of 'quality' high culture. Perhaps we might think of certain performers of easy-listening music as fitting this description. Or in painting, we might think of certain artists who present 'painting for pleasure and profit' programmes on daytime TV. Greenberg would include 'bad' high culture in this definition as well. The melodramatic paintings produced by many artists during the Victorian era would be singled out for particular contempt.

On the other hand, Greenberg also speaks with a mixture of disgust and amusement of that thing to which the Germans give the wonderful name of *kitsch*: 'popular, commercial art and literature with their chromeotypes, magazine covers, illustrations, ads, slick and pulp fiction, comics, Tin Pan Alley music, tap dancing, Hollywood movies, etc.'

The only thing that these otherwise diverse art forms have in common is that they are all manifestations of mass or popular culture, and it seems that is reason enough for Greenberg to reject them. The only thing he leaves standing is something called 'art and literature of a high order' – namely that which achieves the supposedly self-validating status he would outline in 'Towards a Newer Laocoon'. 'High order' culture and kitsch are two separate worlds which cannot be reconciled. Any attempt to blur or cross the boundaries between them can only result in artistic catastrophe.

Presumably, if we do not recognize high-order art when we see it then we, and not Greenberg's sweeping judgements, are at fault. In this respect his posture echoes that of the modernist architects and literary critics we encountered earlier. They all have incredible confidence in their own status as arbiters of taste. They all seem to believe that they – unlike the rest of the 'common herd' – have their finger on the pulse of what is right and good in the field of culture. A postmodernist approach would see this stance as arrogant and deluded.

Some postmodernist criticisms of Greenberg

In the last quarter of a century many criticisms have been levelled at Greenberg and at the general assumptions about art which his ideas represent:

* His art history is too selective.
* This narrative serves nationalistic interests, in that it allows Greenberg to assert the status of American abstract painting and sculpture as a 'world beater'.
* He bases his argument on a simplistic picture of culture as a war between two worlds: avant-garde vs. kitsch.
* He is too prescriptive. He rejects out of hand any alternative ways of understanding works of art. This serves only to mystify art, and to preserve its unreasonably high social status.

In fact, Greenberg's argument undermines its own case: in order to enjoy the *autonomous, purely optical* experience of an abstract painting, you need to have read some modernist theory first.

Andy Warhol

Challenging Greenberg (and the aspect of modernist theory he represented) was central to earlier theorizations of postmodernism in art. But these criticisms have been present in art practice as well as in art theory. (Some commentaries suggest that in postmodern art the conventional line between theory and practice has disappeared.) Many artists could have served just as well, but I will use American pop artist Andy Warhol (1930–87) as an example because his work is well known outside of the confines of the art world.

Most people are familiar with at least some of Warhol's work. His various screen prints of Marilyn Monroe, produced during the 1960s, are very well known, often being reproduced on posters, greetings cards, calendars and so on. His Campbell's soup cans and cola bottles are nearly as famous.

We should also mention Warhol's skill in becoming a media icon, his ability to generate hype, and the way that his art has crossed over into more mainstream culture (postcard and T-shirt reproductions of his best-known images; imitations of Warhol's visual style in adverts). As well as being a hugely successful fine artist, Warhol worked at various points as an illustrator, film-maker and producer, magazine editor, and band manager; contrary to the modernist myth of dedicated struggle with a single medium, Warhol was quite at ease in a range of different roles.

Seeing double: Warhol's postmodern 'hybridity'

In Greenberg's terms, Warhol's work represents a confusion of the arts. It uses popular images and sources within an art context, and semi-industrial techniques in a context that traditionally values original one-offs. It exists between screen-print and painting, original and copy, handmade and reproduced, abstraction and representation, and, most importantly, high and low culture.

Certain aspects of Warhol's work can be made to fit comfortably into Greenberg's prescriptions for modernist painting. It uses unrealistic colour schemes, flat areas of colour and all-over compositions. It is deliberately artificial-looking and makes no attempt to conceal the process of its making.

By producing work that was apparently hospitable to an abstract modernist interpretation, Warhol was able all the more quickly to succeed in the contemporary art market. By seeming to attain certain Greenbergian standards, he soon entered the pantheon of important, highly collectable modern artists.

But unlike the kind of modernism discussed above, Warhol's work was deliberately impure in that it combined these abstract procedures with mass culture images. It provided ordinary, non-modernist people with images they (as well as Warhol) could identify with. As with Charles Jencks' postmodern multivalent architecture, Warhol's art respects the validity of different taste cultures. It is open to the plurality of experiences and understandings that different groups can invest in images. This openness is in marked contrast to the modernist's elitist sense of expertise.

Whether you read a Warhol piece as a criticism of modernism or simply as a picture of a film star – or as both of these at once – depends on what knowledge and experience you bring to it. Against the modernist notion that art is capable of defining itself, Warhol's impure plural coding recognizes that the meanings of art (in fact, the *definition* of art) depend on where it is seen, who sees it, and what mental tools they use in order to read it.

The end of the art world as they know it?

With postmodernism there are no firm rules which can define for us exactly what the limits, purpose and status of art are. Few attempt to create universal authoritative standards (or metanarratives) through which to measure artistic quality, and art appears to have become just another consumer choice.

Some critics have therefore lamented postmodernist developments as a decline in values. The American critic Suzi Gablik has argued that contemporary art no longer has a sense of personal commitment or moral authority. According to her, modernism aimed to bring about the spiritual rejuvenation of the Western world by being uncompromisingly opposed to material values. Postmodernism, on the other hand, is fatally attracted to commerce, mass culture and the assembly-line mentality (Warhol called his studio 'The Factory'). From this point of view, modern-day mass culture is corrupt because it is an instrument of capitalism, and art's job is to oppose it. But with postmodernism, art has been pulled down from its position of spiritual purity and sucked into the orbit of media, advertising and the fetishization of commodities. Opposition to the system is no longer effective. Thus the difference between modernism and postmodernism is that between serious, spiritual art with a moral centre and rootless art which commercialism has drained of meaning and emotional force.

Related but somewhat more nuanced objections to postmodernist art have been raised by the American Marxist critic Fredric Jameson. He has argued that the value of modernist painting lay in its ability to express the alienation, fragmentation and isolation of life brought about by modern society. He refers to a well-known painting, *The Scream* by Edvard Munch (painted in 1893), as a classic example of how modernism uses these themes as part of an adversary, discontented stance towards the modern world. Jameson claims that modernism was always informed by the desire to bring about a better world.

Postmodernism: politically weak?

As in modernist architecture's utopian schemes, 'great' modernist painting was engaged in a search for new ways of living. Postmodernism has abandoned this project. High and commercial culture have collapsed into each other to such an extent that art cannot find a clear position from which to make powerful critical statements about society: there is no longer any real difference between art and advertising.

Critics like Fredric Jameson and Hal Foster have therefore debated whether postmodernist culture criticizes or celebrates the capitalist system. In answer to this question Foster distinguishes between 'resistant' and 'reactionary' forms of postmodernism. The reactionary branch includes figurative oil painting which nostalgically harks back to pictorial traditions. The resistant branch includes photography/media-based art; this is seen as having more critical potential because it can intervene in and challenge the dominant stereotypes and modes of representation of the mass media.

the loss of
the real

Postmodern theory interrogates how representations refer to 'reality'. It does so by looking at how they refer to other representations, and by proposing that 'reality' is both defined and mediated by them. Mass and electronic communications are emblems of the issues which theorists of postmodernism try to describe. The most famous practitioner of this kind of postmodernism is the French cultural theorist Jean Baudrillard. Though his ideas originally grew out of sociological theories, Baudrillard came to take the view that sociological models of reality were too rational to describe the role of representations in contemporary culture.

Central influences on postmodern theory are structuralism and semiotics, which both see meaning as a product of how signs operate in systems of difference. Poststructuralism assumes that these systems are unstable, and emphasizes the role of audiences in generating meanings from signs. The poststructuralist thinker Jacques Derrida's concepts of deconstruction have had particular influence on the fields of literary criticism and architectural theory.

It is sometimes said that theories of postmodernism proclaim 'the end of the real'. While this may be something of an exaggeration, it is true that many of these theories do raise doubts about the relationship between reality and representation. The claim is not quite that nothing is real, but that there is no simple, direct relationship between reality and its supposed expression in words and pictures.

Within theories of postmodernism, these questions are sometimes addressed to relatively recent developments in mass communications and the electronic reproduction and dissemination of sound, image and text. Before the rapid expansion of the internet, television was often central in this area.

On television

Television was an object of academic enquiry and controversy long before the concerns of postmodernism gained currency. There have been many approaches to the scholarly analysis of TV. One trend was concerned with the effects that TV might have on the cultural 'health' of the population. In the 1950s and 1960s, especially, many critics were worried that TV (and other popular forms from paperback novels to rock 'n' roll) posed a threat to both the folk heritage of 'the people' and the high arts. More recent enquiries into the uses and pleasures of popular media have attacked the arguably elitist and patronizing tone of earlier work in this area. In another tradition, many psychologists and sociologists tried to assess the impact of TV on the psychology and behaviour of its viewers, particularly children and adolescents.

From a postmodernist perspective of the sort discussed in this chapter, all of these approaches are too rooted in Enlightenment thinking. In other words they attempt a (supposedly outmoded) rational, mechanical explanation of the meanings and effects of media upon their 'users'. Echoing the concerns of postmodernist and poststructuralist theory, cultural studies has tended to emphasize polysemy and pluralism: meanings are not received uniformly by a 'mass' audience, they are negotiated by many different groups. In light of recent, ongoing developments in television in the digital age (such as multi-platform content, the availability of programmes online and so on), it is likely that television's polysemy and pluralism can only increase.

From a postmodernist perspective, none of the orthodox sociological or 'media effects' approaches to television can provide an adequate account of the area: television resists being described or explained in its entirety. It cannot be contained within a single analytical model. Even within the world of postmodern theory, there has been little consensus about how best to describe television's meanings and functions. This is partly due to the sheer variety of the medium's output. Another difficulty – exacerbated in the age of the internet, digital television and DVD box-sets – is that no researcher can know of all the different audiences for any one piece of content, or of how they might (or might not) respond to it. In this resistance to simplification or generalization, TV has been seen as one of the clearest embodiments of postmodernism.

Another important factor for theorists of postmodernism has been TV's part in the expansion of consumer culture. TV can be examined in terms of its relation to the industrial, economic and technological developments of 'advanced' society. As well as looking at the economic and industrial role of TV in the growth of a new global mass culture, some approaches focus on the content of specific programmes by looking at how particular stories reflect postmodern social conditions.

Finally, TV has been of great importance to researchers offering postmodernist accounts of popular culture. Both aesthetic and social/political aspects of TV may be considered, but the interest lies more in how to look at popular culture in a way which departs from earlier critical perspectives. It is claimed that these earlier, modernist approaches maintained a clear-cut and elitist distinction between high and mass culture. A new, horizontal model of culture is therefore required.

Of course, the angles on TV I have identified above overlap in all sorts of ways. For instance, its visual styles may be linked in complex ways to its industrial and economic attachments.

And this in turn is one of the issues addressed by theorists and researchers who wish to question the established modernist approach to cultural criticism.

TV as postmodern art form?

Style of production

To put it crudely, many modernist, romantic ideas about art stressed the creativity of the individual genius, who was valued for struggling to express his or her unique emotions and insights in his or her chosen medium. With the emphasis very much on the individual at the sharp end of artistic progress it follows that modernism also valued the physical qualities of the work of art itself, and associated these qualities – present in brush-strokes, chisel marks, idiosyncratic stylistic quirks and so on – with notions like 'integrity', 'authenticity' and 'originality'. These values were often thought to signal resistance to capitalism and consumer culture. Putting aside the question of whether these are really adequate ways of looking at art, it should become clear that they do not necessarily apply very comfortably to TV.

Unlike most works of art, a TV programme has no individual creator. Despite the possible talents of particular celebrities, scriptwriters and so forth that go into the making of a programme, and although certain directors do have recognizable styles, the final product is nearly always such a team effort that no single person can be said to have created it. Before our TV receivers pick the transmission up, the programme has been touched by a whole network of personnel, who, even if they have not directly influenced the content of the broadcast, have had some responsibility in making it happen. Hence the way TV is made does not conform to conventional notions of handicraft, or to the familiar picture of the genius pouring his or her innermost thoughts into his or her own work of art.

Style of exhibition

Paintings and sculptures are traditionally thought of as being experienced at first hand by a specific, restricted audience in a specially designed high-culture environment. TV is, by virtue of its style of exhibition, in stark contrast to this. Online, user-generated spaces of display such as YouTube take this aspect even further; in theory anything (including modern art works) can be 'exhibited' for anybody there.

TV programmes and other forms of media content are created by a long chain of personnel, rather than by a single creative being. Similarly, although each item is made only once, it can always make a potentially infinite number of appearances on a potentially infinite number of screens. While paintings and sculptures are traditionally intended to exist as one-offs, each item of traditional broadcast TV has multiplicity built into it. On the one hand, it may be endlessly copied, saved, exchanged and reshown any number of times on videotapes, DVDs, PCs and smart phone apps around the world: to this extent TV content can theoretically be owned by anyone. On the other hand, traditional broadcast media transmit to millions of 'sites' at once and (in this respect like information on the internet) are free of fixed location.

Styles of reception

In the case of conventional forms of fine art, both the architecture of the exhibition space itself and the codes of behaviour supposedly proper to the art world seem designed to encourage a private, one-to-one relationship between the viewer and the work of art. The French sociologist of culture and taste politics Pierre Bourdieu refers to the combination of the physical gallery/museum space and art discourse (i.e. a socially particular genre of language) as a 'field of production'. The presentation of the art work in a pristine, often white room contributes to the feeling that each piece should be attended to on its own terms, uncontaminated by either neighbouring works of art or the outside world.

Conversely there are, potentially at least (and despite the efforts of certain agencies at strict regulation of internet), no such restrictions on where media content can be shown, who consumes it, or how it should be consumed. Unlike the consumption of art there is – again in theory – no established social code or etiquette regarding appropriate viewing behaviour.

Modernism depended on the idea that paintings and sculptures demanded an intent, somehow pure gaze. But TV content – unlike the experience of the cinema – can either be gazed at in fascination, glanced at distractedly while you are doing something else, left switched on while you are in another room, sworn at or argued with, turned up to drown out another noise, or watched for entertainment or education. Schedulers and advertisers might like to imagine you in thrall to the box; it is far more likely that you use TV in a variety of ways for various purposes, and that you fairly often ignore it.

Ways of watching TV: an open-and-closed case

Modernist theories of art fostered the impression that works of art can and should be experienced in their own right, on their own terms, and for their own sake, without reference to other objects in the world. They are regularly presented as though they are permanent, timeless artefacts, requiring no external justification, free of any 'outside' influence. But on TV (and in this way, too, it can be seen as a precursor of the internet), individual programmes and images are not isolated against or surrounded by a neutral ground. They fight for our attention in a crowded – some would say feverish or superficial, others would say exhilarating – environment in which representations proliferate and bounce off each other. They cannot be described in terms of aesthetic purity or self-sufficiency.

We can look in similar terms at commercials, which are often open in the way that they refer to other media products. Many adverts assume that viewers possess a wide knowledge of popular culture, and play on this knowledge by producing a whole range of quotes, in-jokes, parodies, pastiches and imitations of Hollywood movies, TV programmes and other adverts. In addition, they frequently appropriate their soundtracks from any point in the history of popular and classical music, or from world music. Commercials do not attempt to work independently or be seen as self-enclosed wholes, but are explicitly imprinted with – and overtly made out of – their cultural surroundings (one word for these qualities and practices is intertextuality).

It is possible, then, to see TV as the beginnings of a media landscape in which individual items are in various ways open to each other. But this does not mean that they are always correspondingly open to the world. Rather, for some chroniclers of the postmodern, it means that the contemporary mediascape is more like a closed circuit than an open forum. So caught up are media products in chatting among themselves that they have effectively shut the world out.

Welcome to Planet Baudrillard

Jean Baudrillard (1929–2007) has described media culture as consumed by what he calls 'an effect of frantic self-referentiality'. As well as the media now operating without having to make any necessary reference to reality, we now face a situation in which, to Baudrillard's mind, the image 'bears no relation to any reality whatever: it is its own pure simulacrum' (*Selected Writings*, 1988).

Baudrillard has been one of the key figures in the postmodernism debate. Most surveys of the subject see his work as of central importance, and a number of theorists have taken up and adapted his ideas. Although he has actually used the term 'postmodern' only sparingly, his work is often seen to provide especially pungent and mind-bending descriptions of postmodern society. Responses to many of his books and essays, particularly since the late 1970s, have ranged from outrage and bewilderment to uncritical enthusiasm. He has been seen as a weaver of fascinating, elusive texts which play with the (non) meanings of a world engulfed by media. And he has been seen as an infuriating apologist for just about everything that some see as bad about the media and the society that spawned them. In the following reading of Baudrillard we will touch on just part of the work he has done since his first published book, *The System of Objects* (1968).

It is often said that wherever you look, there are images. T-shirts, billboards, posters, packaging, newspapers, magazines, computers, video games, mobile devices and so on can all be listed as sources of imagery. Many of us also own cameras, webcams and camcorders, and most of us are regularly recorded, however unknowingly, by closed-circuit surveillance cameras in shops and high streets. Some proud parents now video their children being born, and many foetuses now put in an early screen preview. For Baudrillard, this apparent obsession with images has fundamentally altered our world.

On its simplest level, Baudrillard's work suggests that all this representation has saturated reality to such an extent that experience can take place only at a remove. We can experience the world only through a kind of filter of preconceptions and expectations fabricated in advance by a culture swamped by images. How, Baudrillard might ask, can you visit, or even live in, New York City without that experience being informed by all the New York Cities you know from movies, TV shows and news reports?

But Baudrillard's writings offer much more than the simple study of media effects. He has looked at a wide range of cultural phenomena from all aspects of contemporary existence and much of his work, rather than occupying any one discipline or school of thought, is best seen as a sort of meeting place for linguistics, sociology, philosophy, political theory and science fiction. The analysis of TV and film, although playing an important part in Baudrillard's work, is therefore just one aspect of his theorization of the postmodern situation.

This situation appears in Baudrillard's work in several guises, and he likes to give it funky yet apocalyptic-sounding names like 'hyperreality', 'implosion', 'cyberblitz' and 'the code'. All of these have fairly different connotations, and their meanings do shift and change throughout Baudrillard's work, but they are all closely related to what he calls simulation. Features of contemporary life as apparently diverse as fashion, environmental design, opinion polls, theme parks, telecommunications and cybernetics have all been rolled together in Baudrillard's hands as manifestations of the single, shiny new regime of simulation.

Dictionaries link simulation to the fake, the counterfeit and the inauthentic. Baudrillard retains these meanings to a certain extent, but pushes them considerably further, so that simulation can no longer be seen clearly as the opposite of truth. We might naturally assume that simulation either duplicates or is emitted by a pre-given real. In this sense we might think that simulation and reality have a necessary attachment to each other. But for Baudrillard, this connection has long since snapped, so that simulation can no longer be taken as either an imitation or distortion of reality, or as a copy of an original. In Baudrillard's dizzying cosmos there is no firm, pure reality left against which we can measure the truth or falsity of a representation, and electronic reproduction has gone so far that the notion of originality is (or ought to be) irrelevant.

Computer-generated images and spaces are the most obvious example of this. They have their own sense of reality (what is sometimes called 'telepresence') which does not depend on the existence of anything outside of their virtual world.

In his 1992 book, *Postmodernism, or the Cultural Logic of Late Capitalism* (expanded from some essays first published in the 1980s), the American critic Fredric Jameson makes a similar point regarding what he sees as the 'depthlessness' of contemporary cultural production. Jameson identifies postmodern 'formal features' in art, architecture, film, video and TV, and finds in them only a superficial cutting and pasting of ready-made images and styles. These are seen by Jameson as signs abstracted from their true origins and reused in meaningless new combinations in the trivial, commercialized space created by mass culture.

The traits are by no means restricted to a single art form. In the realm of moving images alone many critics have found similar qualities in rock videos, advertising campaigns, TV programmes and films like Quentin Tarantino's *Pulp Fiction* (1994). In *Pulp Fiction*, we get no sense that Tarantino is trying to portray a real world. We suspect that he knows little about the criminal underworld which the film seems to portray and that he is dealing almost entirely in cinematic signs, quotes and clichés. Yet whether or not you 'get the references' is as irrelevant as which particular songs dance-tracks get their samples from. In Tarantino's film we are not invited to be outraged by acts of violence, and critical responses to the film have tended to shy away from discussing the racist, sexist and homophobic representations in Tarantino's work. The reason for this is that the film seems to put everything in cinematic quotation marks. We hardly take it as showing anything other than a celluloid film world. It makes no attempt at revealing to us how things really are: it is purely about its own intensity, its own effect as a piece of fictional film. The title itself (as it had in the Tarantino-scripted *True Romance* (1993)) seems to signal that it is not to be taken too seriously. *Pulp Fiction* is a case of what Baudrillard calls 'the emancipation of the sign … from any archaic obligation it might have to designate something'.

So what we are presented with in the postmodern mediascape is a matter of circulating surfaces: a zone in which signs can function without having to be plugged in to what we might think of as a fundamental, authentic realm of existence. What we have, says Jean Baudrillard, is a centreless network of communication that endlessly reproduces and cannibalizes its own constant production of simulations, a situation in which the image is a 'phantasm of authenticity which always ends up just short of reality' (*The Revenge of the Crystal*, 1990).

The major paradox in Baudrillard's work is that, while simulations are emancipated from any reference to reality, they are nevertheless firmly embedded in our lives. They may not refer to some natural, unsimulated reality, but they do have very real effects. In the course of one day we might cry along with a weepie, feel thirsty when looking at an advert for beer, have our faith in human nature shaken by the news, be scared silly by a slasher movie, get excited by seeing a celebrity in the street … In these ways we might say that far from being detached in their own little world, simulations are deeply connected to real life.

On Planet Baudrillard, the distinction between simulation and reality has collapsed. In *The Evil Demon of Images* (1987), he calls this a telescoping or implosion of image into reality. We hinted at some of the ways in which this has happened when we noted how images intersect with (and, we might add, enable) certain experiences of the world. It will not surprise you to learn that Baudrillard goes a lot further than this simple observation. In fact, he turns conventional thinking about the 'logical order of the real and its reproduction' inside out, so that images do not just intersect with the real; they precede it, anticipate it, absorb it and produce it. Even with the examples given above, Baudrillard would claim that reality was an 'effect' of representation.

Performing for real

Below are some examples of the Baudrillardian collapse of distinction between simulation and reality:

* One example of 'the dissolution of TV into life, the dissolution of life into TV' that Baudrillard provides in *Simulations* is the prototype 'reality TV' show *An American Family*, a twelve-part documentary edited down from 300 hours of footage and broadcast in 1973. The 'fly on the wall' documentary follows events in the day-to-day life of a typical family. It seems to bear all the marks of authenticity: there is no sense in which we think of the family as actors. These are real people, after all, and we are watching reality unfold in real time, though only as real-life soap. But we wonder to what extent they are playing up to the recording equipment. If you were not there to watch, would there be anything worth watching?

* You are casting your vote in a general election. Is your vote based on some idea of real politics, or is it informed by the endless soundbites, PR exercises, photo calls and live TV debates (complete with instantaneous opinion polls) which make up the political arena today? Can you think of politics in separation from the perception opinion polls and publicity? Is there any distinction to be made between *real* (deep) and *unreal* (shallow) politics? In this example, we could say that image and reality are totally intertwined: notions of true versus false hardly come into the equation.

* When you go food shopping you choose between designer foods, health foods, exotic foods, slim-line foods, sinful foods, luxury foods, natural foods, traditional foods, 'home-made' foods, convenience foods and 'TV dinners'. Is food now ever just food, or is it always attached to a style, a lifestyle, a body image or a social type? Perhaps you base your food-buying decisions on celebrity chefs, or the kind of person you see yourself as. But where did you get this image of yourself from? Can you separate it from the various identities you are sold daily in advertising, fashion/lifestyle/interior decoration magazines and makeover shows, sex technique videos, shop window displays, fitness programmes, pop music?

* Perhaps the clearest illustration of what Baudrillard calls the 'entangled orders' of reality and simulation is the virtual existence of 'residents' in the online world of Second Life. Avatars socialize and participate in group activities. 'Real world' communities (scientists, artists, religions, etc.) also 'meet' in Second Life workplaces, galleries, churches and so forth. Most significantly in terms of the Baudrillardian deconstruction of reality/simulation dualism, they also exchange virtual currency, property and services. 'Pretend' currency is bought with real money in the 'real world' and made and lost in Second Life.

All of these examples demonstrate how (as Baudrillard would see it) the line between simulation and reality has been erased. As Baudrillard would say, there is no way of identifying a real which exists outside of simulation because we live in a society which is structured according to all sorts of beliefs, ideals and blueprints. In short, reality is structured according to codes. Some codes are manifested in directly political ways – in the drafting of bills, the creation and enforcing of laws, and so on. Some are inscribed into concrete institutions – education, industry and prisons, for example. Others appear in less obvious ways – such as entertainment media, consumer goods, architecture and designed environments. Still more show themselves in the constant surveys, polls and questionnaires which classify the population according to their consumption patterns, income brackets, sexual orientations and so forth. None of these codes can rightfully be called natural or timeless, but all can be said to precede the real in the sense that they produce the real social order in which we all participate. And all can be said to feel real in the sense that they affect real people.

Because of the way it suggests that the real is an effect of simulation, it would be easy to discuss all of this in terms of how people are affected or manipulated by various cultural influences. We might, for instance, try to fit Baudrillard into a critical tradition which looks at how people are persuaded or encouraged to be the good consumers that the system requires in order to keep itself going. It might be tempting to try and find in Baudrillard proof of the influence of TV on the supposedly impressionable masses. And we might try to find proof of Baudrillard's theories in those people who apparently write to TV actors, believing them to be the characters they portray.

However, Baudrillard was keen to distance himself from these kinds of reading of his work. The image of people being manipulated or affected is misleading because it suggests that a gap naturally exists between people and the forces which supposedly shape them. In other words, it suggests that people can exist in an independent, fundamentally unaffected state at some point prior to the system coming along and working on them. In Baudrillard's scheme of things, this is not possible. As far as he is concerned, we are always already caught up in the workings of simulation: 'the social contract has become a pact of simulation, sealed by the media and information', so we are always already part of the network. For Baudrillard, nothing is outside of the flow of signs, codes and simulations.

How are we to react to this scenario? What impact does it have on the lives we lead and the artefacts we make and use? Baudrillard's answer is that it generates panic. We desperately try to get out of simulation by producing events, activities, images and objects which assure us of their (and our) reality. In an attempt to compensate for the fading of the real, we make a fetish of the supposedly authentic. We manufacture an 'escalation of the lived experience ... a panic-stricken production of the real and the referential' (*Simulations*).

Baudrillard calls this the hyperreal or more-real-than-real. The following might be examples:

* jogging, weight training, aerobics, body-piercing, bungee jumping, white-water rafting, adventure holidays
* private life going public in talk shows, true-life stories, tabloid exposés, autobiographies
* interactive TV, phone-in surveys, courtroom TV, 'reality' TV, car crash/execution/surgery videos
* giant video screens bringing you closer to the event at stadium concerts, sports venues, party conferences
* digital special effects, surround-sound, virtual reality, high-definition TV and Blu-Ray
* songs, ads and self-help manuals which implore you to find yourself, be yourself, do it your way, express yourself, unlock the real you, find your inner child.

You could add plenty more examples of your own to the list above. They all illustrate Baudrillard's claim that 'when the real is no longer what it used to be, nostalgia assumes its full meaning. There is a proliferation of myths of origin and signs of reality; of second-hand truth, objectivity and authenticity' (*Simulations*). That is, they all attempt to deter, or provide alibis for, the disappearance of the real at the hands of simulation. The Baudrillardian irony, however, is that these attempts to increase the feel of reality are themselves simulations. Their authenticity is a special effect. They are *hyperreal* rather than *really* real.

We manufacture the real because of simulation. So once again we find that the real is not so much given as produced. Which basically means that we cannot win. This is why Baudrillard says that 'images precede the real', and this is why the relationship between the real and its representation is now inverted. The logical order of things might be that reality expresses itself through representations, but this has been turned upside down.

In order to make any sense of poststructuralism, you need to know a little about structuralism first.

Although it has had most impact in the field of literary theory and criticism, structuralism is best thought of as an approach or method rather than as a clearly defined discipline. Structuralist ideas can theoretically be used in any number of different areas and they can be applied to many different kinds of text. Also, although the term 'structuralism' indicates a fairly restricted cluster of themes, there is not a single set of rules to which all thinkers who have been labelled structuralist rigidly stick.

Structuralism is less concerned with what texts are about, and more with how they work. In order to see these mechanisms more clearly, structuralism deliberately plays down any notion of the content of a text (e.g. the moral of a story, the message of a folk tale). Structuralism is about the formalities of *how* texts mean, rather than about *what* they mean.

At the most general level, structuralism brings to the fore a number of questions about meaning, representation and authorship and explores the relationships between language and knowledge. In this respect, it can be seen as part of a widespread preoccupation with language that has affected a great deal of thought (including what we now call postmodernism) throughout the twentieth century. Anglo-American philosophy, in particular, has been dominated by a fascination with language, on some occasions believing that philosophy was ultimately *about* language, and that it therefore had a special ability to sort out any linguistic confusions suffered by other disciplines such as the sciences or political theory.

Three main structuralist themes have influenced the development of postmodernist thought:

1 **We use language to organize – and even construct – reality.** Language enables us to give meaning to the world. Reality cannot be readily separated from the way we represent it, or the stories we tell about it.

2 **Meanings happen only in relation to structures.** No single thing 'gives off' a meaning of its own accord: it does so only through its relationship to other things.

3 **Verbal and written language provides the clearest demonstration of these structural or relational properties of meaning.** Studying how language works can provide an understanding of how all cultural products create meaning.

Saussure

In the postmodern context, these ideas grew largely out of the work of Ferdinand de Saussure (1857–1913), credited as the founder of both modern linguistics and structuralism. In his *Course in General Linguistics* (1916), Saussure sought to examine the process by which language makes sense to us. He argued that in order to understand the workings of language, it was fairly pointless to look for the historical and/or 'natural' roots of particular words. Instead, words should be looked at as interrelated elements within language as a whole.

Saussure departed from previous approaches to the study of language in that he paid attention not to how it evolved over time, but to how it works as a self-governing system in the present. By denying the significance of the history of words (their etymology) and by refusing to look for their bases in nature, he anticipated the postmodern preference for surface over 'depth'.

Words and things

Common sense tells us that the world is made up of independently existing things which naturally fit the names we have given them. This implies, for example, that there is something about a rose which means that 'rose' is inevitably the right word for it. But Saussure implies that there is no direct or causal relation between a rose and the letters R-O-S-E. Any other collection of letters could conceivably have done the job just as well. It is purely a matter of social convention that roses are called roses.

Because there is no natural or inevitable bond between words and things, Saussure saw language as an arbitrary system. From this starting point, structuralist – and eventually postmodernist – theory abandons any question of 'truth' language: it argues that language can never be a transparent or innocent reflection of reality.

A world of signs

Saussure believed that all of culture is made up of signs. That is to say, social life is characterized by the circulation and exchange of forms to which convention has given meaning. A sign for Saussure is simply any device through which human beings communicate to each other. To the extent that anything can have meaning attached to it, this could be taken to suggest that just about anything can be called a sign.

A science of signs

Saussure argued that verbal and written language offered the best model of how signs made meaning through a system of arbitrary social conventions. Linguistics could therefore provide a strong basis for a scientific study of the life of signs in society. This proposed science of signs would be called semiology (or semiotics: the two are more or less interchangeable).

The rules of the game

Structuralism says that language has a system of rules of combination. These rules permit a large number of different words to be created, but only within the limits of the 26 letters of alphabet. Each specific language will have its own laws regarding how letters can be strung together to make meaningful (or even pronounceable) words. We cannot do what we like with letters (or invent new ones) and expect them to make sense to anybody.

Such simple rules of course extend to how words can be put into order to create phrases, sentences, novels, poems, notes to the milkman and so on.

They also extend to all other languages. In the language of clothes, the rules of selection mean that I can feasibly swap wellington boots for snow shoes, but the rules of combination decree that either kind of footwear would look rather too daring if worn in conjunction with a cocktail dress (or on the wrong part of my body).

Structuralism finds that such norms and conventions apply to all aspects of culture. Language in the sense of speech and writing simply provides the clearest embodiment of the principles which govern all sign systems.

Put at its most basic, the sign is defined by Saussure as an object, word, image or whatever, together with its meaning. Put more technically, it is the unit of meaning produced by the relation of a signifier to a signified:

* **signifier:** the material object, the sounds that words make, the letters on a page, etc. For example 'a bunch of red roses'
* **signified:** the concept or mental image to which the signifier gives rise. For example the 'romance' or 'passion' signified by the bunch of red roses.

The signified is what is meant by the sign. The signifier is what means it.

As we saw in the case of the relationship between words and objects, the relationship between the signified and its signifier is arbitrary. For example, there is no 'natural' reason why a bunch of red roses should signify passion – it is solely a matter of convention. Culture has coded roses in this way, and we have come to take this coding for granted.

The arbitrary relationship between the sign and its meaning does not suggest that you can make signs mean anything that you want them to. Individuals can neither invent signs of their own out of nothing, nor read signs in any way they please. Understanding is always in some sense constrained by rules and conventions. It is not down to personal decision that if I send red roses to someone they will most likely interpret my gesture as a romantic (or corny) one. I have not personally endowed roses with romantic connotations; they have been coded well in advance of my own amorous wishes.

So structuralism and semiology argue that the meanings of signs go far beyond individual intention. This insight is significant for the fields of art and literature, since it calls into question the modernist, romantic view of unique, original works of art being created by individual acts of genius. We will look at this question of authorship in more detail later.

Signs of difference

The established difference between 'rose' and 'nose' is what allows a different meaning to be given to each of those otherwise similar words. In the English language the sound 'r' and the sound 'n' are registered as distinct enough to be granted significance. It is conceivable that another language would not recognize the distinction between the two sounds (or would not make it significant). Neither 'r' nor 'n' have much to say by themselves. They get meaning only by virtue of what other letters they are combined with.

Roses signify passion and romance partly because they are not poppies or chrysanthemums.

It is also important that roses are on the preferred side of the arbitrary distinction we make between flowers and weeds. Few people would receive a bunch of weeds as a sign of affection.

These are all illustrations of the structuralist principle that signs mean what they do because of what the structure of language allows. In this view, signs have significance (that is, they are indeed signs) only in relation to language as a whole. Thus Saussure places little weight on isolated signs. His only concern is for relationships between signs within a self-sufficient system of differences. The meaning of a sign is never its own private property but is the product of its *difference* from other signs.

Poststructuralism

We have seen that structuralism asks where meaning comes from. Does it come from the text itself? Does it come from the context in which the text is consumed? Is the reader free to create his or her own meaning? To what degree can the author of a text control how it is interpreted? Does the production of meaning arise from the interaction of these factors? If so, exactly how do they interact?

Poststructuralism continues to ask these questions, but refuses to find a single answer.

Although the word 'poststructuralism' implies that it simply took over from structuralism at some point in history, it is truer to say that, especially in the 1960s, they ran alongside each other and often crossed tracks. Structuralism and poststructuralism form much of the philosophical background of postmodern theory. Indeed, poststructuralism is often seen as postmodern philosophy. This can give the impression that poststructuralism is a single school of thought or academic discipline. In fact, the term is regularly used to unite the work of a fairly diverse group of thinkers, few of whom ever described themselves as poststructuralists. The most important poststructuralist thinker, however, is Jacques Derrida.

Jacques Derrida and deconstruction

As you know, postmodern thought tends to reject the idea of things having a single, basic meaning. Instead, it embraces fragmentation, conflict and discontinuity in matters of history, identity and culture. It is suspicious of any attempt to provide all-embracing, total theories. And it rejects the view that any cultural phenomenon can be explained as the effect of one objectively existing, fundamental cause.

Derrida (1930–2004) is one of the most influential figures in this postmodern turn of thought against originals, centres and foundations. In a long series of extremely demanding books published since the mid-1960s, Derrida has developed his own particular poststructuralist blend of philosophy, linguistics and literary analysis. It goes by the name of deconstruction.

Derrida's deconstructive work is very much a part of the project of questioning what we might call the meaning of meaning.

It continues the structuralist task of looking for the conditions which allow texts to be meaningful, and it shares their interest in the relationships between language and thought. However, in common with the poststructuralist topics we have discussed so far, Derrida is much more interested in how the meanings of texts can be plural and unstable than in fixing them to a rigid structure.

Conditions of knowledge

If your doctor started to rhapsodize over the aesthetic properties of a rash on your neck instead of offering a proper diagnosis of it, you would probably feel that they were finding the wrong kind of 'meaning' there. But this is not to say that their 'reading' of your rash is simply false, or that it is a misinterpretation of the facts. Rather than being inaccurate, it is simply out of place. Criteria from the field of art are being transported into the field of medicine. In other words, your doctor is going too far outside the confines of medical discourse. Meanings always have a place.

This is an example of how, as Derrida argues, fields of knowledge always put a necessary limit on what can and cannot be validly said. Any discourse – medical, artistic, legal or whatever – is defined by the methods and understandings it makes available to its practitioners, and as such prevents meanings from ever spinning off in inappropriate directions.

According to Derrida, particular disciplines present meanings and truths as obvious. In fact, though, what counts as meaning or truth is determined by the limitations of the discipline which supposedly 'discovers' and describes them. One of Derrida's projects is to show that all meanings and truths are never absolute or timeless, but are always framed by socially and historically specific conditions of knowledge. So when your doctor finally gets round to offering a diagnosis of your rash, he or she is actually bringing into play a great number of particular ideas about what counts as an illness, how symptoms relate to diseases, what doctors are for, and what constitutes medicine.

None of these things are outside of history and culture. Likewise, what is prescribed as a cure will depend on current conditions of knowledge, and these may well be subject to change (a cure today can turn out to be a poison tomorrow).

Of course, none of these issues enters into your conversation with your doctor. You will just want to get your prescription and go home. Consulting your GP for medical advice simply seems like a perfectly normal thing to do, and neither you nor your doctor is therefore likely to discuss the field of medicine as a social construct. The field of medicine, we might say, involves certain historically particular notions of illness, symptom and cure. It also depends on certain Western ideas about scientific rationality and objectivity. For example, modern Western medicine presents itself as a science and thus as fundamentally opposed to magic. All fields of knowledge structure themselves around touchstones of their own making in this way, yet fail to draw attention to their process of construction.

Deconstruction discovers hidden assumptions. There is, it argues, no 'pure' knowledge outside of society, culture, or language. Lyotard similarly proposes that all knowledge, whether scientific, historical or philosophical, is a 'language game'. No facts are finally knowable: there are no truths, only interpretations. History is narrative. This means that all belief systems, however 'rational' they may appear (Derrida has nothing less than 'Western metaphysics' in his sights) are available for critique. The more a point of view presents itself as 'natural' or 'normal' the more Derrida wants to deconstruct it.

Against presence

Thinking of things in terms of what they 'really mean' is a habit of thought which seems perfectly natural to us, and it is hard to imagine an alternative to it. For example, I am writing here about a group of texts as if they form a single body of work which belongs to a single author (Derrida) and in which we find certain basic themes. I have also mentioned postmodernism as if it represented a single slab of knowledge. If Derrida's work has one aim, it is nothing less ambitious than to dismantle this habit of thought, which he sees as an illusory belief in certainty and presence.

By presence, Derrida means that Western forms of knowledge – in science, philosophy, 'common sense' and so on – build themselves up on certain 'centres' and 'origins'. One of the main concerns of deconstruction is to show that those centres and origins have no basis in reality. They are myths.

Derrida's criticism of presence both develops and argues with Saussure's structuralism. He takes from Saussure the idea that language cannot point outside of itself. In other words, language is a self-referring, self-regulating system. Looking up the meaning of a word in a dictionary merely leads you to another word, which you may also need to look up... For structuralism, you do not need to look outside of a sign-system in order to find meaning: meaning is produced by the internal relationships between parts. Thus structuralism refused to find the source of meaning in nature or in the author.

Derrida and poststructuralism agree with structuralism on this point. They both reject the significance of personal intentions or individual experience in the creation of meaning. What counts for both is not intentional self-expression but the operation of the languages we inherit: the means of representation both exceed and precede decisions made by individual human beings.

But Derrida argues that structuralism fails to develop the implications of this theme. He claims that, although structuralism rejects individuality and nature as the bases of meaning, it still holds on to a depth model of representation and interpretation. In other words, it assumes that you can use structuralist ideas to cut through the surface of a text and get at its true linguistic machinery. It can 'solve' texts. In this way, structuralism changed where meanings were thought to come from, but it still gave meaning a foundation in deep structures. For example, Claude Lévi-Strauss thought he had found a single universal structure beneath all (only superficially diverse) cultures.

Derrida calls this notion of depth the 'metaphysics of presence', and it involves the misconception that things are meaningful before we give words to them. For example, because we have the single word 'postmodernism', we assume that there is also a single thing in existence to which the word corresponds. The term 'postmodernism' has thus in effect given rise to the thing so that we can now find ourselves asking 'what is postmodernism?' rather than the more appropriate question 'what does the word postmodernism do?' Derrida would say that we have succumbed once again to the metaphysics of presence: postmodernism has become an object (a presence) in such a way that we can speak of some things as being more postmodern than others.

It is by reference to such presences that interpretations and theories can claim to represent valid pieces of information. But Derrida's deconstruction seeks to expose how the language used in particular fields both creates the presence through which knowledge can claim to be true, and conceals the means by which it creates this presence.

Two of Derrida's key concepts are 'logocentrism' and '*différance*'. Another example of what Derrida sees as the Western 'metaphysic of presence', logocentrism is the mistaken assumption that speech is a transparent vehicle for the expression of the speaker's thoughts, and that writing offers an approximation of this relationship. Derrida dismantles logocentrism by arguing that both speech and thought are texts, and that they are therefore characterized by '*différance*'.

In the French language the word *différer* means both to 'differ' and to 'defer'. In *Margins of Philosophy* (1972) Derrida has endless fun punning on this. It is not an easy word to define. Derrida says '*différance* is not, does not exist', and that it 'is neither a word nor a concept'. But it relates to the semiotic notion of language as a system of differences without positive terms. Signs always contain traces of each other, and therefore that they have no 'essential' meaning of their own. Meaning is always elsewhere; it is indefinitely deferred, delayed and relayed from one sign to another. Différance is, then, both the passive state of being different and the act of differing ('producing differences').

It is intended to evoke the restlessness of language and the slipperiness of meaning.

Deconstructing opposites

As we hinted in the case of our doctor's hidden assumptions about the clear distinction between science and magic, the sense of presence constructed by fields of knowledge relies heavily on systems of opposition. In this medical example, 'science' is the preferred or dominant term (the presence), while 'magic' is the inferior term against which the scientific can be defined. By putting itself on the 'correct' side of the opposition, science constructs itself as the site of objectivity and truth.

Derrida argues that all thought performs such acts of splitting. Thus we habitually think with such oppositions as private/public, nature/culture, body/soul, objective/subjective. One half of the distinction is always seen as inferior to, derivative of, less than, disruptive of or expressive of the other half, which in this process gets privileged as the primary presence. There is always a bias towards one term over the other, and this becomes the assumed grounds for argument, interpretation and proof.

Arguments about the nature of postmodernism often act in a similar way. Whether for or against postmodernism, they often set it up (as the word itself suggests) in terms of its relation (of opposition/continuity, etc.) to a notion of modernism. In this way, modernism becomes unitary, created in retrospect by its supposed 'post'. In this process both modernism and postmodernism come to define each other. Arguments about what postmodernism is, or what its effects are, can then proceed on the basis that it differs in some way from something that it has itself helped to make.

One major point of deconstruction, then, is to analyse the workings of binary oppositions. In doing so it aims to highlight, and criticize, the wider power structures in which binaries are embedded. For example: many modernists oppose high culture and mass culture. In this opposition, 'mass' culture is high culture's monstrous 'other'. Hence the 'high' rejects the 'mass' as 'alien' to itself, but needs it for its own sense of identity (it defines itself through a construction of difference). Moreover, any list of the 'essential' characteristics of one side of the divide (e.g. high culture as active, mass culture as passive) will include features you are just as likely to find in the other. So 'high' is defined by its not being 'mass', and 'mass' is defined by its inferiority to 'high'. Since both *are* what they *are not*, neither has an essence.

Trying to apply a similar approach to such other binaries as West/East, good/evil, light/dark, civilized/primitive or us/them makes the political possibilities of deconstruction apparent. For this reason Derrida has proved useful to postcolonial theory and to some feminist thinkers.

Inside out/outside in

In order to make this book make as much sense as possible, I have had to hold back a great many difficulties and contradictions. I have had to make all sorts of decisions about what to include and what to exclude. I have had to draw relatively firm lines around different points in history, and between different theoretical points of view. On the other hand, I have had to suggest continuities, influences and ongoing trends, where you could just as easily find fracture, conflict and diversity. Finally, I have constantly had to decide how far back to go in tracing the history of an idea, and how far away from the supposed crux of the issue I should go in explaining various strands and influences.

So this book gets its identity from the mass of things I have decided *not* to write about. If I put some of these rejected aspects back into the text (if I made different choices about what is and what is not crucial) you would have a different book in your hands.

All texts, and not just introductory ones, work in the same way to create an illusion of coherence. Deconstruction shows that this is a very precarious illusion.

When Derrida deconstructs a text, he goes for details which give away this process. He brings into the foreground the very things that the text pretends it does not need. He looks for what he calls the present absences, or productive silences. Sometimes he analyses the footnotes of books in more detail than the main thrust of the argument. Footnotes are bits of added information, little pieces of disagreement or possible contradiction which the author leaves outside. To let them back in again would upset the main body of the text, would mess up the argument, and so this is precisely what Derrida's deconstruction does.

postmodern identities

The complexity of life within postmodernity brings about a greater awareness of the various social roles and identities offered to us in consumer culture. This awareness accelerates the demands on the notion of the self that were made in modernity. Postmodernism suggests identity is something fabricated 'on the outside', and that all the faces you show to the world are defined as well as scattered by social forces. These ideas suggest that where the self is concerned, no clear distinction can be made between public/private, inner/outer, authentic/inauthentic.

Humanist ideas of individuality are a product of modern Western systems of knowledge. These came into being with the birth of the human sciences in the age of the Enlightenment. Hence, discourse of the self such as psychiatry, criminology and sexology, might categorize and objectify and define us. Meanwhile postmodernism's interrogation of identity challenges ideas of both self-expression and political action.

Many different models of a 'postmodern self' have emerged from the idea of the social self. But a certain cluster of different questions keep recurring:

* What is the relationship between private and public or inner and outer selves? Is it possible to differentiate them in any clear way?
* Is the self whole, unified, singular? Or is it more appropriate to speak of plural or fragmented selves?
* Have postmodernist notions of fluid and mobile identity replaced modernist ideas of the authentic, if hard-won, self?

The changing nature of the self

In his essay 'Popular Culture and the Construction of Postmodern Identities' (1992), Douglas Kellner describes the transition to postmodern modes of identity. His description maps three stages:

1 Pre-modern identity

In pre-modern communities identity is social, but it is not fundamentally beset by doubt or conflict. Identity is stable because it is defined and maintained by long-standing myths and pre-defined systems of roles. You are part of an age-old kinship system. Your thought and behaviour are enclosed within a limited world view, and the direction your life is going to take is more or less determined for you. Thus there is no need to question your place in the world. Identity is not an issue.

2 Modern identity

In the modern period (starting with the Enlightenment), identity enters into crisis for the first time. As in pre-modern cultures, your personal identity is based on your relations with others. It retains a degree of stability, but its orientations and determinants start to multiply. Whereas in pre-modern communities you knew what your place was in the clan, modern societies begin to offer a wider range of social roles. As Kellner puts it, 'one is a mother, a son, a Texan, a Scot, a professor, a sociologist, a Catholic, a lesbian – or rather a combination of these social roles and possibilities.'

There are therefore expanded possibilities for what you can be. It becomes possible to start choosing your identity, rather than simply being born into it. You start to worry about who you really are and what you should be doing with your life. With this new self-consciousness about who you are, could be or should be, you become more desperate to achieve a successful identity.

There is still assumed to be a real, innate self underneath the public roles you play, but it is a struggle to find it and be true to it. Hand-in-hand with these widespread concerns, philosophers also begin to question the nature of the self, and as time goes on the questions become more anxious. Sigmund Freud and psychoanalysis go in search of the roots of the self and find them caught between unconscious instincts and the bourgeois family. At the same time, the discipline of sociology is developed and insists that all identities are social and that they have to be studied in terms of how they interact in specific social situations.

3 Postmodern identity

Social life is faster and more complex than it was in modernity. More and more demands are placed on us, more and more possible identities are paraded before us, and we have to juggle a rapidly expanding number of roles as society starts to fragment and cultural spaces proliferate.

Some theorists looked at how the selves achieved under modernity have vanished in the wake of consumerism, mass culture, and growing bureaucratization of life. Others propose that the fixed, unified self has always been an illusion. Although identity remains an issue in day-to-day life, postmodern theorists have binned any notion of the self as substantial, essential or timeless. In place of the earnest modernist search for the deep, authentic self, we have a recognition, and sometimes a celebration, of disintegration, fragmented desires, superficiality and identity as something you shop for. In postmodernism the self is without substance, as fashion statements, shopping and lifestyle choices push authenticity out of the equation.

The stylization of life

Commentators like Kellner approach the postmodern self by arguing that certain social conditions have produced in people a heightened sensitivity to appearance and style. In following this line of enquiry cultural theorists trace how the making of identity has become increasingly related to what we buy (or want to buy). We now forge our identities by using goods as signifiers for both individuality (difference from social groups) and solidarity (a sense of belonging to other social groups). In this process identity has been freed from its 'pre-modern' foundations, for as David Harris explains in his book *A Society of Signs* (1996):

> **As the consumer market is flexible and more dynamic than the older ways of regulating identities, much more fluidity is apparent: people can change their identities more frequently, experiment with them, select more options from a cultural supermarket with far less commitment than before.**

Identity in the city

Postmodern theories of identity are often addressed specifically to city life. As such, they are based on ideas about urban lifestyles which have been present since the early days of the modern metropolis. In this respect postmodern attitudes can be said to amplify rather than radically depart from experiences and conditions which have been in place for over one and a half centuries. Because of this apparent continuity, much recent writing about the postmodern city intensifies themes originally developed by early theorists of modernity.

The sources of the modern forms of society noted by Kellner are usually found in the explosion of large-scale urban experience that took place in the middle of the nineteenth century, when over half of the population of England began to live in cities. This soon became the normal course of events as the process of modernization spread across the world. The modern city seemed to concretize problems about the relationship between the individual and the collective. With the growth of the city life was felt to be fragmentary and fluid. This could be exhilarating. But individuals, as we have suggested, also became more self-conscious about their way of life, more concerned about their social role, and more anxious about their place in the world.

In his essay 'Postmodern Virtualities' (1996), Mark Poster argues that postmodernism involves the emergence of novel forms of identity. According to Poster, modernity idealized rational, centred individuals (he cites the 'reasonable man' of law and the educated citizen of democracy as examples), but postmodernity gives birth to a new subjectivity that leaves the 'narrow scope of the modern individual' trailing far behind.

From telephone and radio to video and 'multimedia' the technologies of communication have brought about 'new configurations of individuality': whereas modernists defined themselves in relation to the city, postmodernists are constructed through centreless global or transnational networks of information technology. In this second media age we increasingly deal with other people through communications systems that transform 'the way identifications are structured' and demand new ways of speaking and acting. The cyberspace of the internet is the most radical demonstration of this.

Cyberpeople

The human subject has become a blip: ephemeral, electrically processed, unreal.

(Scott Bukatman, in Annette Kuhn (ed.), *Alien Zone* (1987))

The last two decades have seen an explosion of interest in the fusion of human beings and electronic technology implied by the above quote. This interest has been expressed in both cultural studies and scientific publications as well as in computer games, comic books and science fiction novels. Films such as *Bladerunner* (1982; Director's Cut 1993), *The Terminator* (1984) and *The Matrix* (1999) have caught the imaginations of both cinemagoers and cultural commentators. Although there are many different variations on the idea of a technology–humanity union, and although the phenomenon is far from new, the figure of the 'cyborg' and current developments in information technology have recently received a great deal of attention.

The term cyborg (from 'cybernetic organism') was first coined in the 1960s, when it originally described the kind of body–machine combination necessary for humans to endure long periods in outer space. However, it has become common to use the word 'cyborg' to mean just about any recent variation on the theme of the robot, android or automaton.

The most important feature of the cyborg, whether real or fictional, is its fundamental ambiguity. Many critics have noted that the cyborg either redraws or eliminates conceptual boundaries between mind and body, human and non-human, natural and artificial, inner world and outer world, biological and technological. In doing so, it forces us to ask questions about how we define terms like 'humanity' and 'selfhood'. In this way the cyborg appears to exemplify the claims of postmodernist theory.

It has been claimed that in cyberspace we can escape from our real physical selves, become whoever we wish, and experiment with sexual identities at our leisure, unconstrained by the limits of either flesh or location. In this cybersex revolution we are offered the possibility of performing different sexual identities. There is also the chance not only of swapping, but getting outside of gender.

Postmodernism's fascination with surfaces applies to identity as much as to art, architecture or film. Identity here is a collage assembled from, and fragmented by, any number of cultural codes and contexts. It can be cyborg-like, fluid, nomadic, hybrid, performed, and in a perpetual state of 'becoming'. As such, postmodernist identities can offer escape from supposedly oppressive conventions and stereotypes of gender, nationality, ethnicity, class, sexuality and so on. Or at least it can enable us to 'perform' those readymade identities ironically.

The work of postcolonialist literary critics like Homi Bhabha (e.g. *The Location of Culture*, 1994) and philosophers like Gilles Deleuze and Felix Guattari (e.g. *Anti-Oedipus: Capitalism and Schizophrenia*, 1977) are very different examples of this deconstruction of identity. The American post-feminist critic Donna Haraway (e.g. *Simians, Cyborgs and Women*, 1991) borrows from the fantasies of science fiction to suggest that cyborg-like hybridity might provide the model for bodies and identities liberated from the shackles of oppressive gender codes once thought to be 'natural'. Another American post-feminist academic, Judith Butler (e.g. *Gender Trouble*, 1990), similarly rejects essentialist appeals to 'nature' in her readings of gender and sexuality as performance, masquerade and simulation. One possible criticism of these ideas of ironic, performed and masqueraded identities is that they fail to address the oppressive conditions in which we may sometimes be compelled to 'perform'.

You will never know the real me: Madonna

Of all the superstars who inhabit popular culture, Madonna (1958–) has attracted a volume of critical interest almost equal to the volume of recordings, videos and other materials she has sold. Madonna has remained an icon for postmodern theorists and popular audiences alike.

It has often been implied that Madonna's status was produced in large part from the way she wilfully deployed images of (her own?) sexuality. It seems that as soon as any woman does this, she finds herself in the middle of a fracas, and Madonna was no exception. People have wanted to know whether she represents a forward or backward step for feminism. They have argued about whether Madonna subverts stereotypes or reinforces them.

In his book *Media Culture* (1995) Douglas Kellner argues that the many images Madonna projects of herself defy any attempt to pin her down to a single meaning. He offers an overview of the career-long spectrum of guises in which Madonna has 'imaged' herself,and finds that they only add up to contradiction, multiplicity and enigma. As Madonna herself said of her supposed documentary, *In Bed with Madonna* (a.k.a. *Truth or Dare*, 1991): 'You could watch it and say, I still don't know Madonna, and good. Because you will never know the real me.' Not surprisingly, it proves impossible to present the Madonna 'narrative' as a coherent sequence or story of evolution.

For some critics the Madonna phenomenon represents the worst excesses of commercial exploitation. She is a typical product of cynical media manipulation and her millions of fans are the dupes of a capitalist conspiracy. Such scorn is not uncommon where popular culture is concerned, and it often gets poured down on the pop music industry with particular venom. Even critics drawn to the way Madonna uses multiple images of sexuality and fantasy are sometimes doubtful of her motives. Kellner concedes that many of Madonna's videos are interesting for how they represent minority points of view. But he finds that her apparently subversive tactics are really just attempts to 'appeal to' as many segments of the population (e.g. ethnic minorities, gay people, working-class girls, heterosexual men) as possible, and thus to increase sales by offering a little of something to everyone. Madonna exploits our culture's objectification of the female body for her own material gain. By presenting herself as a sexual spectacle, she helps to maintain the importance that our sexist culture places on the appearance of women.

But Madonna has been important to postmodernism for her ability to plunder the conventions of sexual and gender representation, and thus to show them all up as social constructs. In other words, she 'denaturalizes' sex and gender and encourages us to play with the constructs in any way we find pleasurable. Madonna's message is that the variety of roles provided by today's culture allows identity to be as plural and playful as you wish.

Thus Madonna pushes questions about the politics of identity into a broad public arena in a way that could hardly be achieved by avant-garde art or highbrow theory.

Identity as construction

Postmodernism questions the relationship between public and private models of identity, suggesting that the relationship between inner self and outer appearance is not simply one of expression. In other words, public identity does not simply express what you are really like, deep down.

These reflections can be formulated as postmodernism's 'anti-essentialist' or 'constructionist' views of identity.

Anti-essentialism

This is opposition to the idea that people have a timeless, universal core which ultimately explains their actions. Anti-essentialism has been a hotly debated topic within recent feminist theory, where it has often seemed necessary to stress the idea of gender as a cultural rather than natural category. Given that attempts are sometimes made to define men's and women's 'proper' place in terms of what is supposedly natural it has become important to dispute the way society habitually calls upon an idea of 'nature' as the ultimate explanation of things which happen within culture.

Constructionism

There are really two versions of this:
1 Instead of being born with a particular in-built substance, we become what we are through being acted on by a series of social factors. You are constructed by the social and are ultimately determined by it.
2 We can more or less freely fabricate our identities for ourselves. We have a degree of choice about how to represent ourselves.

These two versions of constructionism are in considerable tension with one another. For this reason, arguments over postmodernist accounts of the self often repeat old philosophical debates about free will versus determinism. For our purposes it is safe to say that personal identity is formed out of the tension between the two, and that this tension can manifest itself in different ways as we enter different circumstances. Postmodernists would reject any attempt at a single, unified and universal theory of selfhood and would look instead at how the determined and the free versions of self-construction interact with and affect each other in variable ways according to our changing social situations.

The invention of man

Discussions about the self in postmodernism are often conducted with reference to the work of Michel Foucault (1926–84). Foucault wrote elaborate histories of social institutions as diverse as the penal system, psychiatry and the social sciences. He believed that no such institutions were neutral or independent, and argued that it was politically necessary to examine how they were tied to the complex operations of power in our society. This power is exercised through surveillance, monitoring and other forms of regulation of people's lives.

For Foucault, the modern-day notion of the self is bound up with the workings of social structures and institutions. This means that none of us can claim to stand apart from the exercise of power. But Foucault does not provide a theory of how naturally free human individuals are oppressed from above by the laws of any one dominant class or group. Instead he proposes that humanity is an idea that has a history: 'the archaeology of our thinking demonstrates clearly that man is a recent invention, perhaps also approaching his end'. To approach Foucault's often demanding work there are at least two heavily used terms that you need to grasp. These are 'the subject' and 'discourse'.

The subject

Within much postmodern theory, and within the critical tradition from which it often draws (notably structuralism and poststructuralism: see Chapter 3), people do not come into the picture very often. In this body of work, the person is often replaced by the subject.

In day-to-day speech, when we talk of being 'subjective', we mean that we are basing our ideas on personal experience, that we are seeing things from our own point of view, and perhaps that our ideas reveal a certain amount of prejudiced self-interest. This is close to one definition of the subject simply as a thinking and feeling, conscious self.

The idea of subjectivity (i.e. being a 'subject') has been applied in many different ways by different theorists and so it cannot be said to have a single meaning. Generally speaking though, as theorists like Foucault use the term, a subject means not simply a conscious person, but a specifically social fact, a being which is at least partially *subjected* to socially produced constraints and divisions. Thus Foucault tends to deny the subject any internal substance. For him the distinction between public and private selves implied by 'human nature' is a false or at least irrelevant one. The subject cannot be reduced to individual consciousness; there are only practices or techniques of the self.

For Foucault, definitions of the self are given only in the social relations we live by. The self is political and knowledge of it is connected to power.

Discourse

Like the subject, discourse can have many different meanings according to who is using it. While it can sometimes designate little more than a general realm of representations, it more often refers to specific social institutions and disciplines. We might speak of the discourse of literary criticism, for example, because literary criticism is both a particular way of putting language to use (e.g. writing criticism) and a discipline (literature) formed within a particular institution (academia). Discourse as Foucault tends to mean it involves all aspects equally – the institution, the discipline and the language use all go together. One enables the other.

Discourses can be seen as controlled systems for the production of knowledge. Though regulated, they are not completely closed systems and have to allow for change and limited dissent. For example, literary critics will disagree over the quality of a particular poem or the meaning of a particular play, but this will not threaten the discourse of literary criticism itself. Indeed, such internal disagreements are crucial in keeping the discourse up and running. Nevertheless, discourses put a limit on what is sayable at any one time: they define what counts as 'legitimate' or 'illegitimate' statements.

Let's talk about sex

We are used to thinking of modern society as something which causes us to repress our instinctive sexual desires. The demands of modern life, its laws and its censorship all conspire to keep our sexual liberty under lock and key. We harbour all manner of dark desires, but the conventions of the modern world prevent us from releasing them. This repression causes misery and even illness. Discovering your true sexuality can bring fulfilment and liberty.

This is what Foucault, in his three-volume *History of Sexuality* (English translation, 1980–6), dismissively calls 'the repressive hypothesis'. He believes that the widespread idea of repression is something of a myth. He argues that, far from being repressive of sexuality, modern Western society actually produces sexuality in the form of endless sex-talk, sex-study and sex-theory. Rather than being silenced, sex since the supposedly repressed Victorian age has grown in importance, and become a serious object of study. It has become the subject on most people's lips. The discourses of sex are constantly multiplying.

Discourse does not free sex: it invents it. Discussion and examination do not liberate sexuality: they make it into a problem. This is because the discourse on sexuality creates the notion that sex is an absolute, abstract category. Sex and sexuality have become the titles used to cover all bodies and their pleasures. Sex is now conceptualized as the drive which motivates all human activity, a dark secret, a deep mystery. So it is no longer enough to simply create bodily pleasures for their own sake. All bedtime (or anywhere, anytime) activities are now sexualized, in the sense that they are seen as manifestations of a single, sexual foundation common to all of humanity. All bodily pleasures are now understood in terms of the degree to which they deviate from, conform to, improve, or avoid sex. Sex is the dominant term, the standard against which 'the body and pleasure' are measured.

And in our own society it is heterosexuality which provides this standard. Homosexuality, some 'aberrant' sexual practices, and so on, might be tolerated, but they are still identified by their difference from the heterosexist norm. Rather than assume that a category like 'homosexuality' simply challenges the norm, Foucault suggests that we should look at the formation of the category itself – how and why it is produced and maintained in specific cultural circumstances. The invention of a norm enables society to define and therefore to marginalize some sexual practices as 'perverse', and thereby to prove the naturalness of heterosexual monogamy and the family values upon which mainstream society bases itself. In short the invention of the 'other' or perverse allows and supports the invention of 'normality'.

Sex discourse 'discovers' and classifies an ever-expanding encyclopaedia of preferences, gratifications and perversions. It creates a realm of perversion by discovering, commenting on and exploring it. In bringing sex into being as an object of study, discourse categorizes and objectifies those who occupy what has been made into the secret underworld of 'deviance'. People no longer own their pleasures: they become specimens of well-documented sexual types instead. Our sexuality and our selves have been turned into a problem, and by constantly encouraging us to talk about it, the discourse on sexuality ropes us into looking for the solution: 'We must ... ask why we burden ourselves today with so much guilt for having once made sex a sin.'

The fiction of expression

If the self is decentred, multiple or fractured, and if personal identity can be seen as fundamentally social, as postmodernists insist, what then do we mean when we speak of people expressing themselves? What are the implications for our long-established notions of artistic genius and originality?

We are used to thinking about art and other forms of cultural activity in terms of these notions. For example, the belief that the value of Van Gogh's paintings resides in the way they capture his supposed insanity in oil paint is a clear case of how we habitually associate the meanings of art with the self-expression of the geniuses who create it. Similar views are found in popular ideas which circulate about eccentric bohemian artists and temperamental creative types. As well as painters, poets and composers you can find this image of the artistic personality in TV documentaries about fashion designers and rock musicians. The fad for releasing restored 'Director's Cut' versions of films, along with the treatment of certain directors as superstars in their own right, similarly shows that although most films are made collectively, we tend to see directors as the ultimate originators and 'explanations' of the films which bear their names.

There has been an explosion of cultural production which seems to manage without the guiding hand of a genius. For example:

* *Music*. In music we have the common practice of sampling in rap, hip-hop and various forms of electronica. There is also scratching and mixing as a form of musical customization or bricolage. The availability of digital sequencers and other computerized pieces of musical equipment has made it easier and cheaper for relative beginners to make high-tech recordings.

* *Architecture*. In architecture, there have been signs of a move towards collaborative projects and away from the virtuoso performance of the master architect.

* *Art*. Following the tradition of Andy Warhol's pop art many recent artists have reproduced ready-made objects, images and other works of art. There has also been some willingness among artists to work collaboratively and to employ assistants to fabricate their work.

All of these practices have been called postmodernist, and this is largely because they are said to subvert modernist ideas about the significance of the author in the making of the work.

The French critic Roland Barthes (1925–80) was one of the figures who helped to formulate a postmodernist view of authorship. Associated mainly with structuralism, semiotics and poststructuralism, some of Barthes' work sets out to question how meaning is produced in works of art. He asked: How are meanings related to their authors? And what is the role of the audience in 'finding' or 'making' these meanings?

The death of the author

In 1968 Barthes published a short essay called 'The Death of the Author' in an obscure Parisian literary journal. In 1977 the essay resurfaced in an English translation in a collection of Barthes' essays called *Image – Music – Text*. Its original publication in France had caused a few ripples in the world of literary theory, but its reappearance a decade later brought it to a much larger audience.

It very quickly became something of a canonical piece, widely quoted in books and university courses on critical theory. The notion of the death of the author also made an impact in the world of art, where it was often referenced in relation to the kind of work mentioned above.

Barthes criticizes mystifying models of authorship on three main counts:

'The birth of the reader must be at the cost of the death of the author'

The normal idea of how meaning works assumes that three steps are taken. First, there exists in an individual author an idea, experience, sensation or mental state. This occurs in the author independently of any verbal or visual language. It does not signify anything yet. It just is. This is close to what we mean by the moment of inspiration. Second, the author shapes inspiration into meaning by manipulating a particular medium. In other words, his or her inspiration is put into signs (words, images, etc.).

Third, these signs convey the meaning given by the author and an audience is able to read them. The meaning as it occurred in the author can be read off the signs.

This model of meaning assumes that the author occupies the centre of the work and is the dominant source of meaning. The text is simply a vessel for meanings which are poured into it by the author. Language therefore simply carries meaning. The role of the reader as an interpreter of the text is essentially to receive meaning and not to create it.

But Barthes reminds us that any text can exist in any number of different times and places unforeseen when the author originally conceived it. A text moves through history, geography and culture, constantly gathering new meanings and revising old ones as it goes. Yet when critics focus on the image of the 'genius' who produced the work, they try to restrict the changeable nature of meaning: they attempt to make the meanings of the text seem more timeless, fixed and universal than they really are.

Elsewhere Barthes notes that 'a text's unity lies not in its origin, but in its destination'. A text is an incoherent mass of signs until a reader binds them together in a way which lends them coherence. The most common way of binding them together, as we have seen, is in the shape of the author. But there is no reason to suppose that there even should be anything coherent about a text. By ignoring what Barthes calls the 'tyrannical' notion of genius, you give the signs more freedom to play, and you liberate the reader to invent new meanings. So the 'destination' of a text is its moment of being read. Of course, there can never be only one such destination, and the author has a very limited amount of control over where the text goes and what people do with it.

'The text is a tissue of quotations drawn from the innumerable centres of culture'

Barthes suggests that all writings are intertextual. One way of understanding this term is as a sort of environment of texts in which an author works and from which she or he draws. Whatever 'original' idea an author might have, certain conditions must be in place in order for these ideas to 'happen'. An important aspect of these conditions is the fact that his or her text, and even the desire to produce it, exists inescapably in relation to a vast number of other texts, mostly by other authors. So no text sits in a vacuum or speaks its own tongue. Authors have to get their ideas from somewhere, and readers can only read in the light of what they have seen before.

Certain artefacts are very noticeably intertextual. That is to say, they overtly refer to other texts. Many spoof films, for example, are intertextual in the sense that they obviously make all sorts of references to other films. Modernist novels like James Joyce's *Ulysses* (1922) also self-consciously refer to other writings. In *Ulysses*, Joyce reworked the themes of Homer's *Odyssey* and played with all sorts of styles, from Chaucer to modern-day beauty-advice columns.

But in fact *all* texts are intertextual. In all acts of authorship, no matter how small, we draw from a repertoire of codes, conventions and influences. If I were to carve a pair of initials and a love heart into the bark of a tree, for example, that act would have been informed by all the love hearts on trees I have seen represented before. And those representations would themselves echo countless other ways of picturing affection. And so on, down an infinite chain of influences and references.

Thus intertextuality is not so much a matter of style as a structural property which allows readers to read and texts to be produced. A text only gathers meaning because it is, as Barthes says, 'woven entirely with citations, references, echoes, cultural languages'. It is both inscribed with the traces of the texts that have gone before it, and formed in the act of reading by the bank of references we all carry with us as participants in culture. The reading of a text is always allowed by knowledges and expectations produced in our 'intertextual landscape'.

'It is language which speaks, not the author'

What Barthes is arguing against here is the taken-for-granted view that ideas spontaneously occur in the mind of the author, as if from nowhere, and are secondarily put into words or other signs. This conventional view suggests that there is a pure realm of ideas which exists prior to language, and that we can simply freely choose the best signs with which to express those ideas.

From Barthes' perspective, there are a couple of major theoretical problems here:

1 You cannot have an idea without it already reaching you in the form of signs. You cannot have a language-less thought.
2 Language is therefore active: it speaks. Signs produce, rather than passively mirror, meaning.

For example: a Monet painting does not innocently capture the fleeting effects of sunlight on a boating lake. We have simply learned to read the signs in such a way that they produce (rather than reflect) that image for us. A very different example: the clothes and behaviour of a person do not express individuality, they make it. The notion of expression suggests that meaning (in this case, individuality) is simply there, waiting for the appropriate signs (in this case fashion and body language) to come along and embody it. But there is not an 'individual identity' until certain clothes and behaviour have been adopted. Their expressive qualities are not invented out of the blue. They work because our culture has encoded them in certain ways. In a sense it is the whole of culture, not the 'author', which is speaking. Thus meaning does not travel *from* a vacuum *to* a sign. The sign *is* the meaning.

Identity politics in fractured times

Do postmodernist theories of identity have any political repercussions? In order to approach this question it is important to note that thinkers like Baudrillard and Lyotard do not regard political, social and cultural affiliations as defined by a rigid, economically based class system. Social class is cut across and fractured by gender, ethnicity, religion, age, sexual orientation and so on. Cultural identities produced in relation to the consumption of 'image' (fashion, music and so forth) may also displace social class as the bedrock of identity. Affluent members of contemporary consumer culture are more able to experiment with tastes, images and lifestyles than ever before, and as a result they are less likely to gather around or recognize themselves in 'class' formations. As the post-Marxist thinker Ernesto Laclau has put it, 'class struggle is just one species of identity politics, and one which is becoming less and less important in the world in which we live'.

Claims about economic determinism (i.e. that all social or cultural phenomena are driven by economic forces) have come under increasing pressure. It seems unlikely, for instance, that the achievement of financial equality would hasten the end of sexism, homophobia, racism or ageism. People are now more concerned with fighting over specific issues than they are with party politics. Voters often possess a portfolio of possibly incompatible values rather than follow 'tribal' adherence to this or that political party. Hence cultural and identity politics have seemed to push class war away from the heart of political activism.

While metanarratives (e.g. atheist fundamentalism) are constantly being reasserted, there seems little reason to believe that in today's infinitely complex transnational societies any one will 'win' or gain dominance over all others. Hence Lyotard argues that there can be no great blueprint which will bind all 'language games' together. Preferring the idea of chaos to that of progress, Lyotard repudiates the Enlightenment project by picturing a world in which all overarching belief systems collapse, and no concept assumes more than a partial value. Truth is a short-term contract. It is no longer viable to speak in the name of universal human principles and expect them to form a fixed standard by which to judge other people's perspectives. It is impossible to represent the world in such a way that everyone would recognize their own knowledge and experience.

For postmodernism, difference is preferable to agreement because it is from difference that invention arises. The lines should always be kept open: consensus should be discouraged because consensus 'does violence to the heterogeneity of language games', as Lyotard says. Universal principles suppress cultural diversity. The only way to avoid 'violence' to different experiences, identities and expressions is to forget the prospect of unity and to dismantle any institution which aims at 'governing the social bonds'.

In its distrust of 'totalizing' thoughts or actions postmodernism has a libertarian aspect. Despite their demystification of genius and originality, thinkers like Lyotard often place individual creativity at the centre of their philosophy. Critics of postmodernist theory question the political usefulness of this stance. Postmodernism's celebration of fragmentation and difference can, for example, be seen as a rejection of Marxism because it seems to strike at the heart of socialism's faith in collective action.

Postmodernism does not reject politics, but takes a modest (some would say defeatist) view of what counts as political action. Rather than investing in some grand Utopian project of total human emancipation, postmodern politics suggests that it is more worthwhile to challenge power on an everyday level. Hence Lyotard suggests that we can all fruitfully engage in small-scale acts of dissent which 'gnaw away at the great institutionalized narrative apparatuses ... by increasing the number of skirmishes that take place on the sidelines'. Everything from defacing billboards to flash-mobbing can be seen as an attempt to virally attack the powers-that-be or disrupt the social system.

But however empowering identity politics may be at a 'grass roots' level, many critics have expressed doubts. It can be argued that the play of postmodernist identities is merely a sideshow within the current stage of capitalism, and a distraction from the reality of class struggle. As the philosopher Slavoj Žižek outlines the problem, 'the postmodern identity politics of particular (ethnic, sexual and so forth) lifestyles fits perfectly the depoliticized notion of society'.

In other words, it can be argued that postmodernism represents little more than the triumph of consumerism. Complying too readily with the market, postmodernism is fatally seduced by commodities, fashion and the mass media. Theories of free-floating signifiers, simulation, hyperreality and language games provide no conceptual support for political practice or decision making.

Irony, cultural relativism and the exhaustion of Enlightenment reason seem poor grounds for making political or ethical choices.

The humanist ideal of a globally valid ethical code may be unattainable, but we still need to distinguish right from wrong. The theoretical issue is how to assert the 'rightness' of our right while acknowledging that it is conditional upon our cultural context. Universal truths may be a useful fiction.

Post-postmodernism?

It has been suggested that the greatest virtue of the term 'postmodernism' is its lack of precision. Although it has been around for a long time, it still refuses to settle into a single meaning. As we have seen, one of postmodernism's recurring themes is this very instability of meaning: meanings, it is argued, are never unified; they are at all levels disrupted by difference and uncertainty. To this extent we might say that postmodernism practises what it preaches. In doing so it allows ideas to stay mobile, constantly reinventing themselves and adjusting to changing circumstances. Because it is about finding new ways of describing the world, we can regard it (as Jurgen Habermas said of modernity) as unfinished. It can be seen as an ongoing project to find new ways of looking at new times.

So it is difficult to write a conclusive conclusion for this book. Because so many of the topics we have addressed remain open-ended, there is no simple way of closing the case. Theorists like Derrida, Baudrillard and the rest would at any rate suggest that this is how it should be, and would resist the idea that their work can be summarized in one easy package. Nevertheless, that is what I have tried to do.

Certain matters are, of course, no longer 'hot'. Pluralism in the art world, for example, is rarely debated today. Similarly, the 'blurred' distinction between high and low culture now seems normal rather than novel. Indeed, thanks to postmodernism, terms like 'high culture' are now difficult to use without irony. These are not signs that postmodernist conditions have disappeared. On the contrary, it may be that we are now more thoroughly 'in' postmodernism than ever. Seen in this light, the debates of the 1970s and 1980s seem like a period of transition: changes were observed and were often resisted; 'modernists' clung to ideas declared obsolete by 'postmodernists'. The dust generated by these disputes has now settled. 'Postmodernism' may no longer be the most fashionable label for our times, but nothing has yet replaced it. It may even be that 'incredulity towards metanarratives' is now so widespread that finding one name for 'our times' (*whose* times?) seems an impossible task.

Yet many of the problems and conditions that postmodernism identifies are likely to persist. In some cases they will intensify. The conflict between local and global cultures and the issues of cultural difference now seem more urgent than ever. Information technology and the 'mediascape' continue to expand. New ways of commodifying our lives are constantly being discovered in ways thinkers like Baudrillard and Jameson could never have anticipated. Developments in genetic science and artificial intelligence ensure the relevance of postmodernist debates about the limits and nature of the self. You can easily add to this short list.

It can therefore be said that claims to have reached the 'end' of postmodernism are not only premature, but distract attention from some of the important challenges it lays down. However slippery and contradictory it might be, and however tired the word might now be, postmodernism can still offer ways into worthwhile debates about contemporary societies, cultures and lifestyles.

Printed in Australia
AUHW010613260722
366732AU00009B/40

9 781444 123197